God's Suffering Servant

9 ACTIVITY BOOK

Suzanne Kauffman

Illustrated by James Converse

To accompany *God's Suffering Servant* by Eve MacMaster

Herald Press
Scottdale, Pennsylvania
Kitchener, Ontario

This Story Bible Activity Book includes instructive activities for Christian families, congregations, and schools to use with their children.

Prepared by the Congregational Literature Division of the Mennonite Publishing House. Director, Laurence Martin; editor, Marjorie Waybill. Consultants: Eve MacMaster, Linda Hess, Marlene Kropf, Barbara Rogers, Donna Hernandez, Pat Young. Tested in twenty-five congregations (large, small, rural, urban, and inner city) and family settings.

GOD'S SUFFERING SERVANT ACTIVITY BOOK

International Standard Book Number: 0-8361-3450-8
Printed in the United States of America

92 91 90 89 88 87 10 9 8 7 6 5 4 3 2 1

Contents

A Message for Parents and Leaders

This Story Bible Activity Book is meant to be used with *God's Suffering Servant,* the ninth of the Story Bible Series written by Eve MacMaster, along with your favorite translation of the Bible. It includes activities which Christian families and communities of faith can use to educate their children in the stories, memories, beliefs, and values of their biblical heritage. The activities are numbered to correspond to the stories in *God's Suffering Servant.*

Reading or telling the Bible story is the crucial leadership function. Following the story students will be ready for the activities. Each session begins and ends with group activities. While group activity 1 may be worked at individually, it is important to check and discuss the answers together as a group. In addition to the group activities where are activities from which students may choose according to their ability and interest. Grade-level differences will be minimized as persons of various ages work both together and alone.

While the target age for the activities is the intermediate-age child, it is not limited to this age-group. Students who are developing their reading skills will have difficulty with some activities unless there are persons willing to help them understand the activity.

An answer key appears on pages 55-60. If the leader prefers, the key may be removed before giving the book to the student.

Basically, four kinds of learning activities are included:

1. **Knowledge.** Activities which help the students demonstrate their knowledge of the story.
2. **Experience.** Activities which invite students to respond with their personal choices or expressions of feelings.
3. **Discovery.** Activities which extend the story by searching for greater depth in the story or additional topics.
4. **Memory.** Activities which focus on meaningful memory of songs or Scripture.

This activity book provides opportunities for students to respond to the stories. It will help them remember the stories and experience God speaking to them, calling them to a life of faith and obedience. In this way they too will become part of the ongoing story of God and his people.

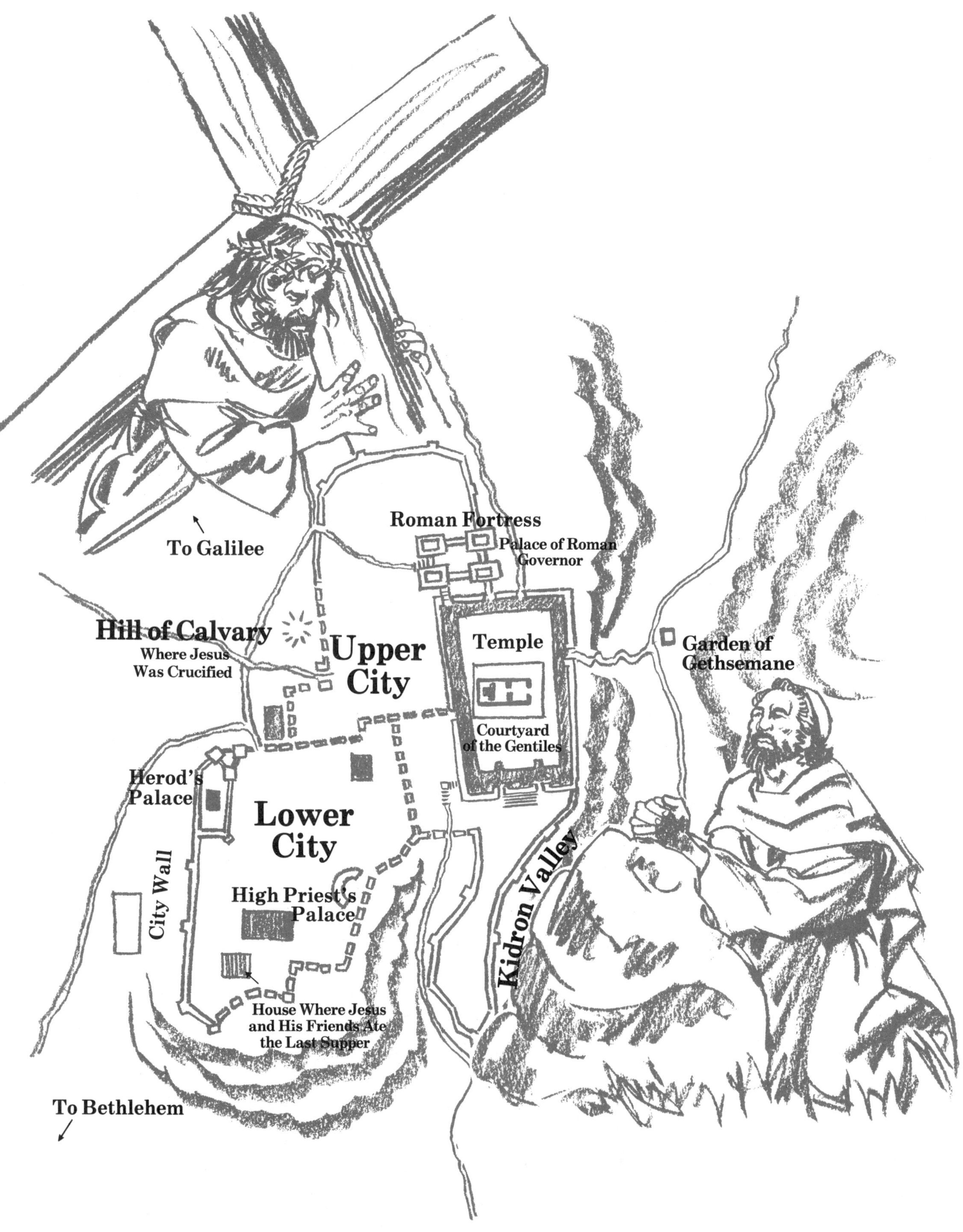
Roman Fortress
Palace of Roman Governor
To Galilee
Hill of Calvary
Where Jesus Was Crucified
Upper City
Temple
Garden of Gethsemane
Courtyard of the Gentiles
Herod's Palace
Lower City
City Wall
High Priest's Palace
Kidron Valley
House Where Jesus and His Friends Ate the Last Supper
To Bethlehem

1

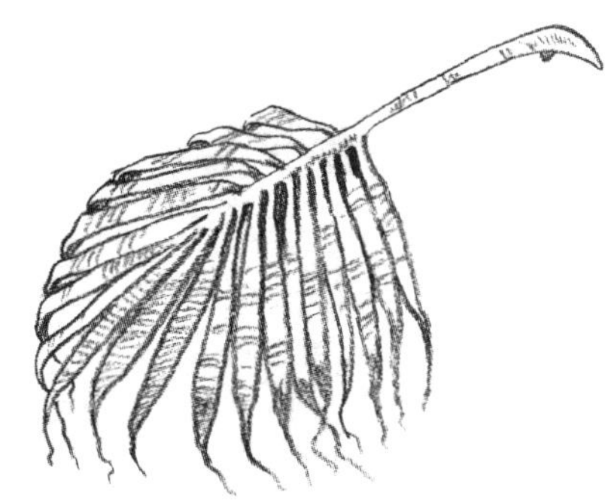

Your King Is Coming!

Group Activity 1

Matthew 21; Mark 11; Luke 19; John 12

Put the events of the story in chronological order on the timeline by placing the appropriate letters above the notches.

A Jesus sent two of his disciples into a village to get a young donkey for him.
B When Jesus reached the place where the road went to the Mount of Olives, the large crowds began to sing.
C Jesus looked at Jerusalem and said, "O Jerusalem! If only you understood the message of peace."
D Because the praises of the people made the religious leaders unhappy, they asked Jesus to quiet his followers.
E Some of Jesus' followers spread their coats on the donkey's back.
F Some people in Jerusalem wanted to make Jesus their king.
G The people of Jerusalem were excited because Jesus was coming to Jerusalem for the Passover Feast.
H Two men questioned the disciples as they untied the donkey.
I Jesus rode the donkey into Jerusalem while the people shouted praises to him and waved palm branches.
J Jesus told the religious leaders that if his followers were quiet, the stones would praise him instead.

___ / ___ / ___ / ___ / ___ / ___ / ___ / ___ / ___ / ___
1 2 3 4 5 6 7 8 9 10

Did You Know?

- Hosanna means "save us now" and is also used as a cheer.
- Palm branches were a sign of Jewish freedom.
- Clothes spread on the road were a sign of a king coming.

Using the word hosanna write an acrostic to describe Jesus and how the people felt about him as he rode into Jerusalem. Add letters to make a word or words to describe Jesus and the people on the way.

H ______________________

O ______________________

S ______________________

A ______________________

N ______________________

N ______________________

A ______________________

Expectations

The people of Jesus' time had expectations of Jesus. Who did they think Jesus was and what did they expect of him? Use A=1; B=2; C=3, etc., to learn what these expectations were.

1. __ __ __ __ __ __ __ __ __ __ __ __
16 5 18 8 1 16 19 10 5 19 21 19

__ __ __ __ __ __ __ __ __ __ __ __
23 1 19 20 8 5 15 14 5 20 8 5

__ __ __ __ __ __ __ __ __ __ __
16 18 15 16 8 5 20 19 8 1 4

__ __ __ __ __ __ __ __ __ __ __.
19 16 15 11 5 14 1 2 15 21 20

2. __ __ __ __ __ __ __ __ __ __ __ __
16 5 18 8 1 16 19 8 5 23 1 19

__ __ __ __ __ __ __ __ __ __ __ __
20 8 5 12 5 1 4 5 18 23 8 15

__ __ __ __ __ __ __ __ __
23 15 21 12 4 19 1 22 5

__ __ __ __ __ __ __ __ __ __ __ __ __
20 8 5 13 6 18 15 13 20 8 5 9 18

__ __ __ __ __ __ __.
5 14 5 13 9 5 19

3. __ __ __ __ __ __ __ __ __
16 5 18 8 1 16 19 8 5

__ __ __ __ __ __ __ __ __ __
23 15 21 12 4 4 18 9 22 5

__ __ __ __ __ __ __ __ __ __ __ __
15 21 20 20 8 5 18 15 13 1 14 19

__ __ __ __ __ __ __ __ __ __ __
1 14 4 19 5 20 21 16 20 8 5

__ __ __ __ __ __ __ __ __ __ __ __.
11 9 14 7 4 15 13 15 6 7 15 4

God's Anointed One

How did Jesus' actions show that he was God's anointed one? To answer this question write the letter of the alphabet that comes just before each letter found below.

1. I F B M F E U I F T J D L.

__ __ __ __ __ __ __ __ __ __ __ __ __.

2. D B T U P V U E F N P O T.

__ __ __ __ __ __ __ __ __ __ __ __ __.

3. P Q F O F E U I F F Z F T

__ __ __ __ __ __ __ __ __ __ __ __ __

P G U I F C M J O E B O E

__ __ __ __ __ __ __ __ __ __ __ __ __

U I F F B S T P G U I F

__ __ __ __ __ __ __ __ __ __ __ __

E F B G.

__ __ __ __.

4. S B J T F E B N B O

__ __ __ __ __ __ __ __ __ __

G S P N U I F E F B E.

__ __ __ __ __ __ __ __ __ __ __.

Group Activity 2

1. Did the people of Jerusalem recognize Jesus for who he was? Can you think of any examples of times God visited you, your family, or your congregation in a special way and you didn't realize until later that it was God?
2. The people were singing and shouting hosanna to Jesus as he rode into the city. Talk about how you would welcome Jesus if he came to your town today.

2

A House of Prayer for All Nations

Group Activity 1

Matthew 21; Mark 11; Luke 17, 19; John 2

Fill in the blanks with words from the story. The letters in the box will spell a word that was very important in Jewish worship.

1. Jesus discovered men selling live _ _ _ _ _ in the temple.
2. These men were also selling _ _ _ _ _ _ _.
3. Those selling live animals were located in the _ _ _ _ _ _ _ _ _ _ _.
4. Jesus became very _ _ _ _ _ when he saw the temple and what was happening.
5. Jesus told the men that they had made his house a _ _ _ _ _ _ _ for robbers.
6. Jesus said, "Stop turning my _ _ _ _ _ _ _'_ place into a marketplace!"
7. The temple authorities wanted a _ _ _ _ from Jesus to show them what right he had to do what he did.
8. Twice Jesus asked the people if they hadn't read the _ _ _ _ _ _ _ _ _ _ _.
9. Jesus told the authorities that he would rebuild the _ _ _ _ _ _ in three days.
10. Even the _ _ _ _ _ _ _ _ _ _ didn't understand that he was talking about his body.

House of Prayer—Hideout for Robbers

List things you can do to make God's house a house of prayer or a hideout for robbers.

House of Prayer	Hideout for Robbers

What Is Faith?

Jesus said, "Have faith in God and you can do the same things I do." What is faith? Give your ideas of faith.

Faith is:

____

____

____

Follow the directions carefully to discover a definition of faith given in the Bible.

"J3 QDVZ FD8JQ 86 J3 BZ 6URZ

____

3F JQZ JQ8KG6 WZ Q3PZ F3R,

____

J3 BZ CZRJD8K 3F JQZ JQ8KG6

____

WZ CDKK3J 6ZZ." QZBRZW6 11:1

____

Change the 3's to O's. Change the Z's to E's.
Change the D's to A's. Change the Q's to H's.
Change the J's to T's. Change the 8's to I's.
Change the 6's to S's. Change the K's to N's.
Leave all the other letters the same.

Angry but Not Too Angry

Jesus became very angry when he saw how the temple had become a marketplace instead of a place of prayer. What do you do when you become angry? Put a circle in front of the ways you express anger. Put an X in front of the ways you feel are good ways to express anger. Remember angry feelings are okay if these feelings make you want to do God's work and are not for selfish wants.

__ Throw a tempter tantrum

__ Yell at your sister or brother

__ Kick the dog

__ Go for a walk

__ Talk to someone abut your feelings

__ Be by yourself for a while

__ Eat a snack

__ Talk to the person who is making you angry

Group Activity 2

1. Share your answers to "What Is Faith?" with a friend.
2. Discuss ways in which anger can help you do God's work.

3

Jesus Teaches in the Temple

Group Activity 1

Matthew 21—22; Mark 11—12; Luke 14, 20

Who said it? Write the first initial of the person speaking before their words. Some may be used more than once.

A. Jesus
B. King
C. Temple rulers
D. First Son
E. Second Son
F. Landowner
G. Farmers (tenants)
H. Father

__ 1. "The one who went to the vineyard."

__ 2. "We don't know."

__ 3. "The wedding feast is ready. Invite anyone you can find."

__ 4. "Son, go work in the vineyard today."

__ 5. "This is the son and heir. Let's kill him."

__ 6. "Who gave you the right to do these things?"

__ 7. "John the Baptist showed you the right thing to do, but you didn't believe him."

__ 8. "He'll put wicked men to death and give the kingdom to someone else."

__ 9. "Yes , sir."

__10. " The kindgom of God will be given to people who will produce fruit for God."

__11. "I'll send my beloved son."

__12. "Many are called; few are chosen."

__13. "I won't go."

__14. " Let me ask you a question."

Parables

In the story Jesus used several parables (stories that teach a lesson) to make the people think about the kingdom of God. Earlier he had told them what the kingdom of God was like. Look up the references and write a few words to describe the kingdom of God.

Luke 13:18-19 ____________________

Luke 13:20-21 ____________________

Mark 4:26-29____________________

Matthew 13:24-30 ____________________

An Angry Landlord

Jesus had a special message to tell the temple rulers and those listening to them. So he used the parable of the angry landlord and his vineyard to help them understand God's gift to them and what they were doing to this gift. Use the number code to see what God wanted the people to know.

	2	4	6	8	0
1	A	B	C	D	E
3	F	G	H	I	J
5	K	L	M	N	O
7	P	R	S	T	U
9	V	W	X	Y	Z

__ __ __' __   __ __ __ __ __ __ __
34 50 18 76   76 72 10 16 38 12 54

__ __ __ __   __ __   __ __ __
34 38 32 78   78 50   36 38 76

__ __ __ __ __ __   __ __ __
72 10 50 72 54 10   94 12 76

__ __ __ __ __;
30 10 76 70 76

__ __ __   __ __ __ __ __ __   __ __   __ __ __
58 50 78   12 16 16 10 72 78   56 10   78 36 10

__ __ __ __ __ __ __   __ __   __ __ __
52 38 58 34 18 50 56   50 32   34 50 18

__ __ __ __   __ __   __ __ __ __ __   __ __
94 38 54 54   14 10   34 38 92 10 58   78 50

__ __ __ __ __ __ __   __ __ __   __ __ __ __
76 50 56 10 50 58 10   94 36 50   94 38 54 54

__ __ __ __ __ __ __   __ __ __ __ __
72 74 50 18 70 16 10   32 74 70 38 78

__ __ __   __ __ __   __ __ __ __ __ __ __.
32 50 74   78 36 10   52 38 58 34 18 50 56

Did the people accept God's special gift to them? ____________________

Jesus' Message

Jesus was trying to tell the people something with his parables. Use the number code to discover Jesus' message.

__ __ __ __ __ __ __   __ __ __   __ __
14 10 16 12 70 76 10   98 50 70   18 50

A Verse to Learn

The vowels in this verse are wrong. Correct the vowels and then memorize the verse.

E IM THO VANI, OND YIO ERO THA BRENCHAS. WHIAVAR RIMEONS EN MA, IND O AN HEM, WOLL BAER MICH FREIT FUR YIA CEN DI NETHONG WETHIAT MU.
John 15:5

____

____

____

____

Group Activity 2

Jesus told his disciples that they would bear much fruit if they remained in him. What does it mean to bear fruit? Read Galatians 5:22 and then discuss bearing fruit for Jesus.

4

Jesus Answers His Enemies

Group Activity 1

Matthew 21—22; Mark 12; Luke 20

The missing word in each sentence fits the puzzle. Print one letter in each square.

1. Jesus' enemies tried to ________ him.
2. The ________ followed strict rules and hated the Romans.
3. A picture of ________ was on the coin Jesus looked at.
4. The Sadducees did not believe in the ____.
5. The Sadducees controlled the ruling ________ of the Jews.
6. Jesus asked for a ________ coin.
7. Jesus' ________ were trying to trap him.
8. The ________ cooperated with the Roman government.
9. The Sadducees asked Jesus a question about the resurrection so that he and the Pharisees would look ________.
10. Jesus asked, "Whose ________ is on this coin?"
11. Jesus called the Pharisees and Herodians________.
12. The ________ were another group of leaders who tried to trick Jesus.

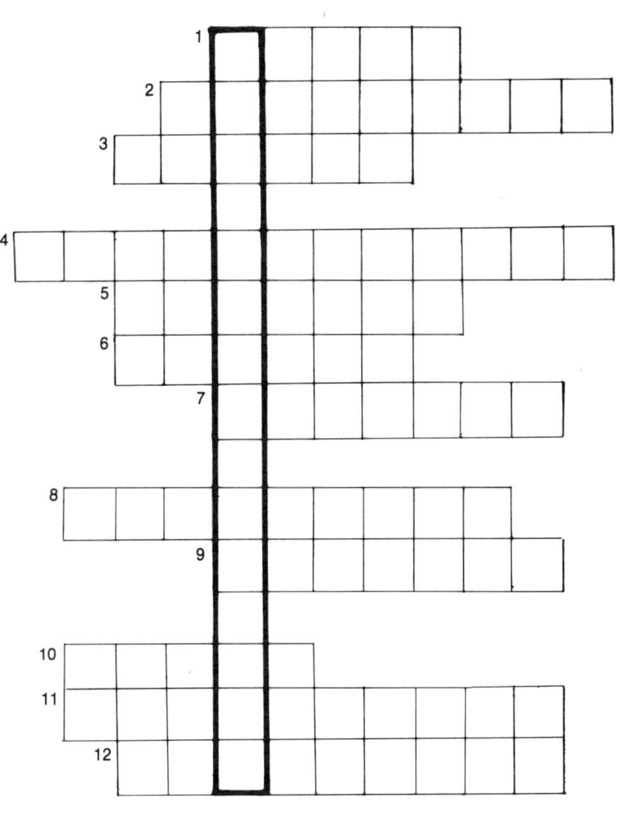

Important Words

Find four words in the puzzle that tell us what is more important than any government.

____

____

Who's Number One?

The way you act and the choices you make show others if God rules your life or whether you're number one in your life. Look at the sentences below. Put an X in the box which best describes you.

	Yes	Usually	Sometimes	Never
1. I do what my parents want me to do.				
2. I do what Jesus wants me to do.				
3. I do what my friends want me to do.				
4. I do what I want to do.				

What Would You Do?

It's difficult to be friends with persons who don't like you or whom you feel don't treat you fairly. Check your response to each of these situations.

1. Your team has just lost an important game. One of the members from the winning team is bragging and making smart remarks to you.
   __Pretend not to hear
   __Walk away
   __Tell him rudely to shut up
2. Your best friend has just won the essay contest which you were sure you would win.
   __Congratulate her on her achievement
   __Walk away in anger and tears
   __Tell her that you would have won the contest, too, if you were the teacher's pet as she is
3. Some of the kids are planning to play a trick on the neighborhood bully. You...
   __warn the bully
   __do nothing
   __ask how you can help with the trick

A Verse to Remember

Sometimes it's hard to let Jesus rule in your life; to let him be number one. This verse will help you when you are having difficulty. Start at the arrow and go around the circle clockwise writing down every third word until you have used all the words. Memorize the verse.

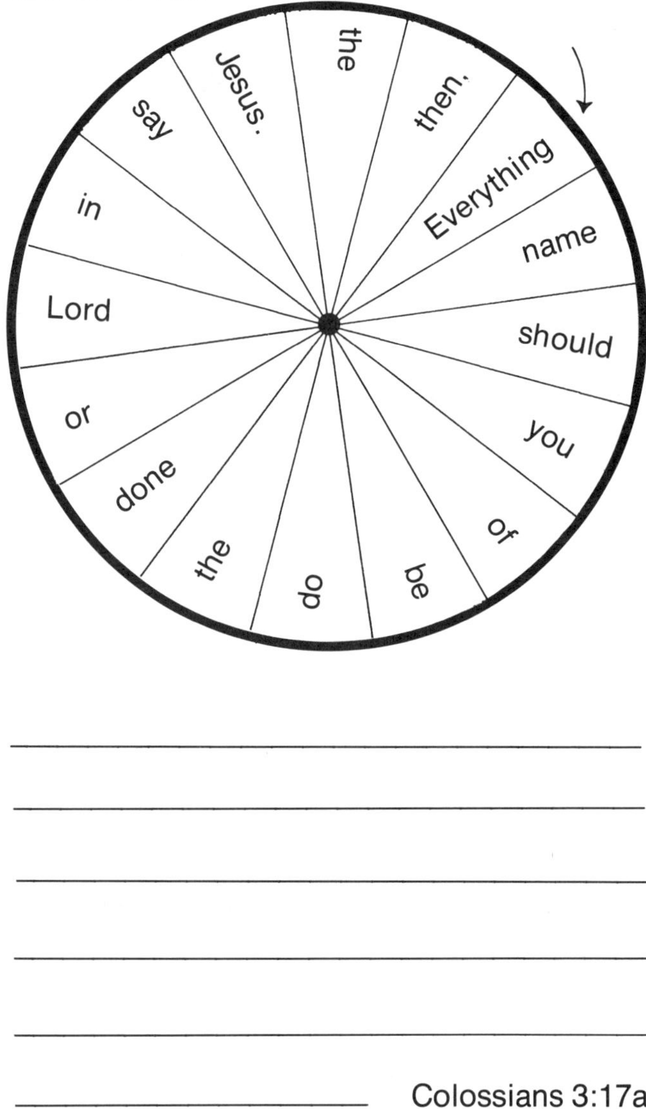

____

____

____

____

____

______________ Colossians 3:17a

Group Activity 2

1. Discuss answers to "Who's Number One?" Decide who is number one in your life.
2. Finish the sentence: God rules in my life by....

5

"Woe to the Pharisees!"

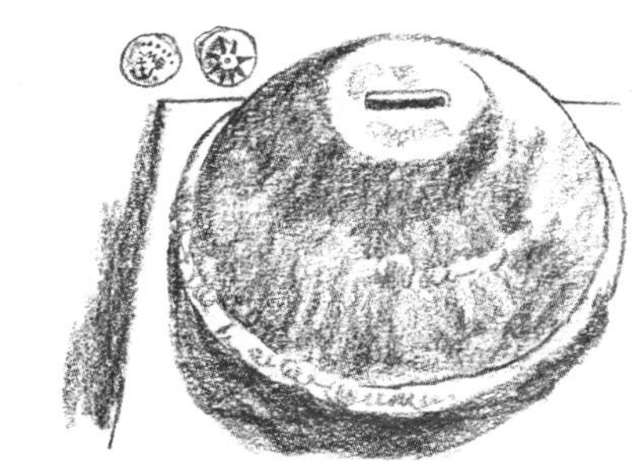

Matthew 23; Mark 12; Luke 11, 20—21

Group Activity 1

Decide if the statement is true or false. If the statement is true, circle the letter under T; if false circle the letter under F.

T	F	
W	N	1. Jesus told his disciples to watch out for the scribes and Pharisees.
O	A	2. The Pharisees practiced what they preached.
T	T	3. Many of the Pharisees wanted to please themselves rather than God.
B	C	4. Jesus was happy with the Pharisees.
E	H	5. Jesus said that the Pharisees were humble and didn't take places of honor.
O	A	6. Jesus' followers are only to call God their Father.
U	P	7. The poor widow gave all she had in the temple offering.
T	H	8. The Pharisees were careful to give only one tenth of everything.
O	!	9. Jesus told his disciples that the Pharisees were good examples to follow.
N	D	10. Jesus said the greatest person was the one who acted like the Pharisees.
O	Y	11. Jesus called the Pharisees snakes and blind guides.

Jesus' Warning

Jesus used the ections of the Pharisees as a warning to his disciples. To discover Jesus' warning first write the circled letters on the lines and then write the uncircled ones.

_ _ _ _ _ _ _ _ _ _ _ _ _ _

_ _ _ _ _ _ _ _ _ _ _ _ _ _ _.

Are You a Phony?

Jesus called the Pharisees hypocrites. A hypocrite (or phony) is someone who wears a mask to cover up the real person inside. What is there in you that is phony? How do you wear a mask? Color the boxes in front of the responses that describe you.

- ☐ I don't let others know I am trying to serve God.
  I say one thing but am really thinking something else.
- ☐ I say what I think people want me to say.
- ☐ I always want my own way.
- ☐ I make excuses when I am at fault and don't want to change my behavior.
- ☐ I'm really friendly to and agreeable with my Sunday school teachers, parents, minister, but I really make fun of them later.
- ☐ I do as the crowd does even if I don't want to or I think what they are doing is wrong.

Will the Real Me Stand Up?

Think about the statements. Answer honestly.

"I feel best about myself when . . ."

"I say one thing but mean another when . . ."

"I don't like myself when . . ."

"I am wearing a mask when . . ."

"I am happiest when . . ."

"I am lonely when . . ."

How to Become a Big Shot

Jesus warned his disciples about acting like the Pharisees who wanted to be great and thought they were better than others. Jesus' value system is different. In God's kingdom who is the greatest? To find the answer you must first decide which letters stand for which numbers.

H=____ M=____ E=____ S=____ T=____

R =____ O=____

_ _   _ _   _ _ _
1 5   B 6   1 7 6

_ _ _ _ _ _ _ _,   _ _ _
G 2 6 A 1 6 4 1   5 N 6

_ _ _ _   _ _ _ _ _
3 U 4 1   4 6 2 V 6

_ _ _ _ _ _.
5 1 7 6 2 4

A Verse to Remember

When you feel like you are more phony than real remember this verse.

_ _ _ _ _ _ _   _   _ _ _ _
1   10

_ _ _ _ _   _ _   _ _,   _   _ _ _,
20

_ _ _   _ _ _   _   _ _ _   _ _ _
30

_ _ _ _ _   _ _ _ _ _ _ _   _ _
40   50

_ _.   _ _ _ _ _ 51:10

Put the letter A in spaces 4, 7, 14, 25, 31, 35, 41, 55.
Put the letter C in space 1.
Put the letter D in spaces 24, 27, 37.
Put the letter E in spaces 3, 6, 11, 13, 20, 33, 52.
Put the letter G in space 22.
Put the letter H in space 12.
Put the letter I in spaces 17, 45, 47, 49.
Put the letter L in spaces 38, 42, 56.
Put the letter M in spaces 19, 51, 57.
Put the letter N in spaces 18, 26, 32, 36, 50.
Put the letter O in spaces 21, 23, 39.
Put the letter P in spaces 8, 28, 44, 53.
Put the letter R in spaces 2, 10, 15, 46.
Put the letter S in spaces 43, 54.
Put the letter T in spaces 5, 16, 30, 48.
Put the letter U in spaces 9, 29.
Put the letter W in space 34.
Put the letter Y in space 40.

Group Activity 2

Choose a friend and share a time when you felt you were wearing a mask. Share also a time when you felt that you were true to yourself and to God.

6

The Fall of Jerusalem

Group Activity 1

Matthew 23—24; Mark 13; Luke 17, 19, 21.

Jesus gave the disciples signs of what was to happen in the end times before his return. List those signs below by putting the letter in the space that comes just after the letter in the alphabet. In this case Z=A.

1. S G D Q D / V H K K / A D
   V Z Q R.

2. S G D Q D / V H K K / A D
   D Z Q S G P T Z J D R.

3. S G D Q D / V H K K / A D
   E Z L H M D R.

4. S G D Q D / V H K K / A D
   S D Q Q H E X H M F
   R H F M R / E Q N L
   G D Z U D M.

5. I D R T R' / E N K K N V D Q R
   V H K K / A D / Z Q Q D R S D C.

6. S G D Q D / V H K K / A D
   E Z K R D / O Q N O G D S R
   Z M C / E Z K R D
   L D R R H Z G R.

7. S G D / R T M / Z M C / L N N M
   V H K K / M N S / F H U D
   K H F G S.

8. S G D / R S Z Q R / V H K K
   E Z K K / E Q N L
   S G D / R J X.

What Next?

Then Jesus tells about a very important event. In your own words describe what comes next.

____

____

____

Jesus' Promises

Jesus promised two things as he was describing the signs that would tell of his second coming. To find out what these promises were, this time write on the blank below each letter the letter that comes just before it in the alphabet.

1. _ _ _ ' _ _ _ _ _ _ _ _
E P O U Q S F Q B S F

_ _ _ _ _ _ _ _ . _ _ _
T Q F F D I F T V T F

_ _ _ _ _ _ _ _ _ _
U I F X P S E T J

_ _ _ _ _ _ _ _ _ _ _ _
X J M M H J W F Z P V

_ _ _ _ _ _ _ _ _ _
U I S P V H I U I F

_ _ _ _ _ _ _ _ _ _ .
I P M Z T Q J S J U

2. _ _ _ _ _ _ _ _ _ _ _
F W F S Z P O F X I P

_ _ _ _ _ _ _ _ _ _ _ _
T U B O E T G J S N U P

_ _ _ _ _ _ _ _ _ _
U I F F O E X J M M

_ _ _ _ _ _ _ .
C F T B W F E

Return Visit

How do you feel when you think about Jesus' coming to earth again? Complete the sentence by checking the responses that describe your feelings. Add one of your own to the list.

Thinking about Jesus' second coming makes me

1. confused
2. happy
3. frightened
4. want to tell more people about Jesus
5. want to live more for Jesus and less for myself
6. want to think of other things
7. bored
8. confident
9. ______________________________

Heavy Stuff

Jesus gave the disciples some heavy stuff to think about. How do you think they felt about Jesus' words. In the balloon describe the disciples' thoughts.

Group Activity 2

1. Suppose you knew Jesus was coming next week. How would you live? What would you do? How would this make a difference in the way you live this week?
2. Share your answers to "Return Visit."

7

Be Prepared!

Group Activity 1

Matthew 24—25; Mark 13; Luke 12, 17, 19, 21

Fill in the blanks and then use the words in the crossword puzzle.

ACROSS

1. Jesus told a __________ about the coming of the Son of Man.
4. There were __________ bridesmaids.
6. Jesus told his disciples to __________ __________.
7. The __________ were placed to the left of the king.
10. The __________ will divide the sheep from the goats.
12. Half the bridesmaids took extra __________ for their lamps.
13. The __________ foolish bridesmaids were out buying oil when the bridegroom came.
14. The bridesmaids took __________ to light the way to go.
15. At the end time there will be a __________ __________.

DOWN

2. Jesus said the righteous will have __________ __________;
3. The __________ were put on the King's right.
5. The bridesmaids were waiting for the __________.
8. Jesus said, "The coming of the __________ ____ __________ will be like what happened in the time of Noah."
9. The __________ bridesmaids went into the bridegroom's party because they were prepared.
11. The sheep will occupy the place to the __________ of the king.
14. The goats will occupy the place to the __________ of the king.

A Warning

Jesus gives a warning several times. The warning is written below, but the vowels are incorrect and the spacing is wrong. Correct the vowels and the spacing in order to read the warning.

"WITCHIE T!BAP RIPIRODYI EDEN'T KNEWTH ADEYIRHE IRWHANT HISIN UFMENW ELLC IMO."

____

____

____

A Verse to Remember

Jesus taught that to really meet the needs of people—to really be a servant—we must love people. But love is more than saying, "I love you." Learn 1 John 3:18 to remember what love involves.

1 John 3:18

Our love should not be
just words and talk;
it must be true love,
which shows itself in action.

What's Your Answer?

Finish the statement. Think about it carefully.

One way I am faithfully serving Jesus until he returns ______________________________

____

____

____

Jesus the Model

Write Jesus' teaching in Luke 6:36 on the lines provided. Then read the story in Luke 18:35-43 and draw what Jesus did. Jesus lived what he taught.

Luke 6:36:" ______________________________

____

______________________________________"

____

Group Activity 2

1. Share experiences when you have shown love to someone whom you felt was difficult to love.
2. Discuss the statement, "God has no hands but our hands." In connection with this discussion share your answers to "What's Your Answer?"

8

Jesus Is Anointed and Betrayed

Group Activity 1

Matthew 26; Mark 14; Luke 22; John 12—13

Decide which is the best answer to finish the sentence. Some sentences may have two answers.

1. Jesus predicted that during the Passover he would be
   a. rescued
   b. crucified
   c. taken to heaven

2. Every day the elders, priests, and scribes made plans to
   a. worship Jesus
   b. kill Jesus
   c. get rid of Jesus.

3. The priests, scribes, and elders wanted their plans to remain a secret because
   a. they wanted to surprise Jesus
   b. they were afraid of the people
   c. they were afraid the Romans would come to take away their power

4. Simon the leper lived in
   a. Jerusalem
   b. Jericho
   c. Bethany

5. While Jesus was at Simon's house
   a. the religious leaders arrested him
   b. a woman anointed him
   c. the disciples were annoyed

6. The woman who anointed Jesus
   a. was trying to become famous
   b. used expensive perfume
   c. showed Jesus she was his follower

7. Jesus' disciples
   a. were annoyed with the woman
   b. wished she would have used the perfume more wisely
   c. thought the woman was foolish for wasting such expensive perfume

8. Judas Iscariot
   a. was a thief
   b. helped himself to the money bag
   c. cared about the poor

9. Jesus told the disciples
   a. to quickly clean up the perfume
   b. to stop being annoyed and let the woman alone
   c. that they would always have the poor with them

10. Because of what she did Jesus promised the woman
    a. that what she did would always be told
    b. lots of money
    c. fame and recognition

11. Judas became angry and upset with Jesus so he
    a. yelled at Jesus
    b. told the chief priests he was willing to hand Jesus over to them
    c. told the other disciples how he was feeling

12. Judas offered to betray Jesus
    a. for thirty pieces of silver
    b. because he did not love Jesus
    c. because he liked money

Costly but Worth It

The woman used very expensive perfume to anoint Jesus. But she knew it was worth it. Follow the directions closely to discover a reason why it was worth the cost.

1.	J	X	Z	E	P	Q	S	B	E	T	T	Y
2.	X	U	S	R	E	D	T	E	D	W	X	A
3.	B	R	O	W	N	S	O	N	E	P	L	E
4.	P	X	A	J	O	S	E	T	W	O	D	B
5.	W	I	X	T	Z	H	F	A	L	L	T	H
6.	T	E	J	I	M	W	O	M	A	N	X	Z
7.	Z	W	S	P	R	I	N	G	H	O	P	Z
8.	S	E	V	E	N	A	P	I	N	K	N	O
9.	M	I	N	R	I	C	H	A	R	D	T	L
10.	E	D	T	E	N	H	A	N	N	I	M	X

1. Cross out the X's in each line.
2. Cross out the color words in lines 2, 3, 8.
3. Cross out the girl's name in lines 1, 4, 10.
4. Cross out the boy's name in lines 2, 6, 9.
5. Cross out the number words in lines 3, 4, 8, 10.
6. Cross out the first and last letters in lines 4, 6, 9.
7. Cross out the Z in lines 1, 5, 7.
8. Cross out the season of the year in lines 5, 7.
9. Cross out the P in lines 1, 7.
10. Cross out the Q in line 1.

____

____

____

Recognition

To discover two things Jesus said to show he was pleased with what the woman had done, start with the first letter and write down every other letter. When you come to the end go back to the beginning and start again.

1. S T H I E F H U A L S T D H O I N N E G A F B O E R A M U E

_ _ _   _ _ _   _ _ _ _ _   _

_ _ _ _ _ _ _ _ _ _

_ _ _ _ _   _ _ _   _ _.

2. W L H D A A T N T D H S I H S E W W O I M L A L N B D E I R D E W M I E L M L B B E E R T E O D

_ _ _ _   _ _ _ _ _   _ _ _ _ _ _

_ _ _   _ _ _ _ _   _ _ _   _ _ _ _ _

_ _ _   _ _ _   _ _ _ _ _   _ _

_ _ _ _ _ _ _ _ _ _.

A Verse to Remember

Memorize Galatians 6:10a. Ask Jesus to help you do what the verse says.

> **Galatians 6:10a**
> So then, as often as we have the chance, we should do good to everyone.

Group Activity 2

You are not able to pour expensive perfume on Jesus, but there are other ways to show him you love him. Discuss and share your ideas.

9

Jesus Washes His Disciples' Feet

Group Activity 1

Matthew 26; Mark 14; Luke 22; John 13

Match the beginnings of the sentences with the correct ending. If you match the beginnings and endings correctly you will discover a name Jesus used to describe himself. Write it on the blanks below the sentences.

____ 1. Jesus told his disciples to follow a man carrying a water pitcher

____ 2. The Passover was celebrated each year to

____ 3. Before eating the meal with his disciples

____ 4. Jesus was giving the Passover

____ 5. The most important Jewish

____ 6. "If the Lord and Master washes your feet

____ 7. When it was time to eat the Passover meal

____ 8. The ancestors of the Jews had put the blood of the Passover lamb

____ 9. Because Peter didn't want Jesus to act like a servant

____10. The Passover lamb had to be young and perfect

____11. Peter wanted Jesus to wash also his hands and face

Endings

T. Jesus arrived at the house with his twelve disciples

R. Jesus washed his disciples' feet

N. with none of its bones broken

V. a new meaning because of what he would do

N. you must also wash each other's feet"

I. he asked him not to wash his feet

S. who would show them where to prepare the Passover supper

A. festival was the Passover

K. on their door frames in Egypt so that the Angel of Death would not stop there

G. when he understood what Jesus was trying to teach the disciples

E. remind the Jews how God had saved them from slavery in Egypt

Jesus called himself a _ _ _ _ _ _ _

_ _ _ _.

Who Me? A Servant?

Jesus tried to show his disciples and his future followers how to be a servant. Use your Bibles to find some of these ways. Match the correct reference with the servant work.

Reference	Servant Work
Matthew 6:2-4	•tell the good news, baptize, and teach
Matthew 6:6-18	•help the needy
Matthew 5:21-22	•don't judge
Matthew 28:19-20	•love God and others
Matthew 25:36a	•care for the sick
Matthew 25:35b	•keep the commandments
Matthew 19:16-17	•show hospitality
Matthew 25:34-35a	•pray and fast in secret
Matthew 7:1	•visit those in prison
Matthew 25:36c	•clothe those who are in need
Matthew 22:37, 39	•don't call people ugly names
Matthew 25:36b	•help feed the hungry

Color It Out

Philippians 2:4 says what Jesus tried to show. Color the boxes (below) containing the letters G and Z blue. Color the boxes with the letters B and C green. Write the remaining letters in order row by row to find the verse. Then memorize it.

A	G	Z	N	G	D	Z	Z	L	B	O	Z
C	O	G	K	C	Z	O	C	Z	U	C	T
F	B	O	B	Z	R	G	B	O	G	N	B
E	Z	A	Z	N	G	O	G	Z	T	G	H
B	E	R	B	S	C	I	C	N	C	T	E
R	B	E	G	S	B	T	S	G	N	Z	O
Z	T	G	J	B	U	C	B	S	B	T	G
Y	G	O	Z	U	Z	R	Z	G	O	W	N

_ _ _   _ _ _ _   _ _ _   _ _ _

_ _ _   _ _ _ _ _ _ _'_

_ _ _ _ _ _ _ _ _, _ _ _

_ _ _ _   _ _ _ _   _ _ _.

A Disciple Search

In the letters find the names of Jesus' twelve disciples as they are written in the story. You will find them up, down, backwards, and diagonally.

J	T	A	A	P	I	L	I	H	P	P	U	J
A	R	N	C	S	J	B	G	L	E	C	F	D
M	G	W	E	M	O	L	O	H	T	R	A	B
E	B	E	B	T	A	O	R	I	E	H	L	N
S	R	R	V	S	M	T	M	O	R	D	J	B
A	E	D	S	E	I	A	T	B	N	S	K	S
M	O	N	B	Y	T	M	S	H	D	R	G	A
O	J	A	M	E	S	T	O	L	E	K	R	D
H	B	L	M	D	C	J	K	N	P	W	C	U
T	O	I	R	A	C	S	I	S	A	D	U	J

Group Activity 2

1. Make job coupons to give to friends and family. On each coupon write the name of the person and the job (for free) you will do for that person. Make one for each family member and a friend.
2. Make a poster with pictures cut from magazines of people serving one another.

10

The Last Supper

Group Activity 1

Matthew 26; Mark 14; Luke 22; John 13

Read each statement; decide if it is true or false. Then follow the directions carefully for filling in the lines on the next page. The lines appear in the activity "Old Versus New."

1. Jesus told Peter that he would deny him (Jesus) three times. If the statement is true write a S in lines 13, 15, 17, 19; if the statement is false write a T in those lines.
2. Jesus told his disciples that he would drink the fruit of the vine again soon with them. If the statement is true write an A in lines 6, 7, 9, 23, 25, 34; if the statement is false write an O in lines 6, 7, 9, 23, 25, 34.
3. During the Passover meal Jesus told the disciples that someone would betray him. If the statement is true, write a T on lines 1, 27, 40; if the statement is false write a C in lines 3, 10, 12.
4. Satan entered Judas when he took the drink Jesus gave him. If the statement is true write a G in lines 3, 12, 29, 31, 36; if the statement is false write an E in lines 3, 12, 29, 31, 36.
5. All the disciples were upset when Jesus predicted that someone would betray him. If the statement is true write an H in lines 2, 28; if false write an A in lines 5, 16, 22, 37, 40.
6. Jesus told Judas to do what he had to do quickly. If the statement is true, write an F in lines 10, 26; if the statement is false write an O in lines 18, 26.
7. John asked Jesus if the one who would betray him was a Pharisee. If the statement is true write an S in lines 33, 38; if the statement is false write an N in lines 30, 37, 39.
8. Jesus told the disciples that the glory of God would be shown through the Son of Man. If the statement is true write an L in lines 5, 24; if the statement is false write a B in lines 5, 24.
9. Jesus told his disciples he really didn't want to eat the Passover meal with them. If the statement is true write an M in lines 8, 14; if the statement is false write an M in line 21.
10. The disciples would not be able to go where Jesus was going, he told them. If the statement is true write a U in line 14; if the statement is false write an F in line 22.
11. Peter told Jesus he would follow him even to prison. If the statement is true write a V in line 35; if the statement is false write an I in line 4.
12. Jesus told the disciples that the one who would betray him was one of the twelve disciples. If the statement is true write a D in line 8; if the statement is false write an E in line 11.
13. The disciples understood why Jesus told Judas to do quickly what he must do. If the statement is true write an N in line 4; if false put a Y in line 20.
14. Jesus broke bread for the disciples as a symbol of his body. If the statement is true write a W in line 32; if the statement is false write a W in line 13.
15. All the disciples agreed that they would probably deny Jesus if given the

chance. If the statement is true write a B in lines 18, 38; if the statement is false write a B in lines 4, 22.

16. The disciples were to meet Jesus in Galilee after he had risen. If the statement is true write a J in line 11; if the statement is false write C in line 16.
17. Jesus predicted that Satan would test the faith of all the disciples. If the statement is true write an A in lines 18, 38; if the statement is false write a V in line 35.
18. The cup of wine was a symbol of Jesus' blood given as forgiveness of sins. If the statement is true write a C in line 33; if the statement is false write an R in line 33.
19. Jesus asked his disciples to forget about what he had told them during the Passover meal. If the statement is true write a J in line 16; if the statement is false write an I in line 16.

Old Versus New

In Jeremiah 31:31-34 God promised a new covenant because the people did not keep the old covenant. The old covenant was the Law given by God. If you did Activity 1 correctly you will discover what the new covenant was. Write the letters on the lines.

___ ___ ___   ___ ___ ___ ___ ___   ___ ___
1 2 3   4 5 6 7 8   9 10

___ ___ ___ ___ ___   ___ ___   ___
11 12 13 14 15   16 17   18

___ ___ ___ ___ ___ ___   ___ ___   ___ ___ ___
19 20 21 22 23 24   25 26   27 28 29

___ ___ ___   ___ ___ ___ ___ ___ ___ ___ ___
30 31 32   33 34 35 36 37 38 39 40

Explore a Maze

Find a message in the maze. Start at the circled J and end with the circled D.

Group Activity 2

11

The Way, the Truth, and the Life

Group Activity 1

John 14—15

Jesus was comforting his disciples. In this story he gave them many promises to help. These are for you as well as the disciples. Use the number code to record the six promises of Jesus.

	2	4	6	8	0
1	A	B	C	D	E
3	F	G	H	I	J
5	K	L	M	N	O
7	P	R	S	T	U
9	V	W	X	Y	Z

1. 38 94 38 54 54 34 50
72 74 10 72 12 74 10 12
72 54 12 16 10 32 50 74 98 50 70.

2. 38 94 38 54 54 16 50 56 10
14 12 16 52 32 50 74 98 50 70.

3. 98 50 70 94 38 54 54 36 12 92 10
54 38 32 10 14 10 16 12 70 76 10
50 32 56 10.

4. 38 94 38 54 54 12 76 52 78 36 10
32 12 78 36 10 74 78 50
76 10 58 18 78 36 10 36 50 54 98
76 72 38 74 38 78 78 50 14 10
98 50 70 74 78 10 12 16 36 10 74.

5. 38 94 38 54 54 34 38 92 10
98 50 70 56 98 72 10 12 16 10.

6. 38 94 38 54 54 58 50 78
54 10 12 92 10 98 50 70
12 54 50 58 10.

The Way to the Father

Thomas asked Jesus an important question. Fill in the blanks. Use the letters in the circles to find Jesus' answer. Memorize his answer.

1. There are many ◯(9) _ _ ◯(3) _ in my Father's house.
2. Jesus told Philip, "◯(7) _ _ ◯(6) _ _ _ has seen me has seen the Father."
3. Jesus promised another ◯(5) _ ◯(13) _ _ _ to be with the disciples.
4. He called the helper the Spirit of _ _ ◯(10) _ _.
5. Jesus called himself the true _ ◯(1) ◯(11) _.
6. The disciples were told to remain in Jesus if they wanted to produce ◯(14) _ _ _ _
7. The _ ◯(2) _ _ _ _ _ _ _ prunes the vine that doesn't produce fruit.
8. The disciples had already been ◯(4) _ _ _ _ _ _ _ by Jesus' teachings.
9. Jesus wanted his disciples to share his _ _ ◯(8).
10. Jesus told the disciples not to worry if the _ _ _ _ ◯(12) hates them because it had hated Jesus first.

_   _ _   _ _ _   _ _ _,
1   2 3   4 5 6   7 2 8

_ _ _   _ _ _ _ _,
4 5 6   4 9 10 4 5

_ _ _   _ _ _   _ _ _ _.
2 11 12   4 5 6   13 1 14 6

Jesus Gives Hope

Jesus gave the disciples much to think about, hope for, and encouragement. To read what Jesus said, start at the top brick and write down every other letter. The first two words are done for you. When you reach the bottom go back to the top and use the remaining letters.

D
E O
M N Y
O O T U
B B E E W
L O I R E R
V I E E I D N
A G N O D D U B
P E S L E I T E J
V E E S A U L S S T
O O I L N D M T E H .

"D O   N O T   _ _ _ _ _ _ _ _

_ _ _   _ _ _ _ _ _ _," _ _ _ _ _

_ _ _ _   _ _ _ _ _ _ _. "_ _ _

_ _ _ _ _ _ _   _ _ _   _ _ _;

_ _ _ _ _ _ _   _ _ _ _

_ _   _ _."

Group Activity 2

1. Choose one of the verses from "Jesus Gives Hope" or "The Way to the Father" to memorize. Put it on a card, decorate it, and put it where you can read it often. Soon you will have it memorized.
2. Discuss ways to show love
   - in school
   - in the home
   - in the neighborhood
   - to those who are hard to love
   - in the world

12

Jesus Prays for His Disciples

Group Activity 1

John 16—17

Complete each sentence using words from the word list. Then write the letters from each answer in the spaces of "Another Message."

love	world	disciples
understand	sorrow	brave
good	alone	keep
guide	away	joy
glorify	evil	with

1. Jesus' ___ ___ ___ ___ ___ ___ ___ ___ ___
   (32, 16 45, 42)
   believed that Jesus had been sent by God.

2. Jesus said he would go ___ ___ ___ ___
   (1 10 4 7)
   for a while.

3. The disciples did not
   ___ ___ ___ ___ ___ ___ ___ ___ ___ ___
   (9 5 6 15 14 2 21 22)

4. Jesus promised the disciples that their
   ___ ___ ___ ___ ___ ___ would turn to ___ ___ ___.
   (29 27 40 37 31) (28 24)

5. Jesus said his going away was for their
   own ___ ___ ___ ___ so that the Holy Spirit
   (47 8 25)
   could come to ___ ___ ___ ___ ___ them.
   (26 18 23)

6. Jesus told his disciples that in the
   ___ ___ ___ ___ ___ they would have sufferings
   (44 37 33)
   but they should be ___ ___ ___ ___ ___.
   (35 20)

7. Jesus said he was never ___ ___ ___ ___ ___
   (13 46 39)
   because the Father was always
   ___ ___ ___ ___ him.
   (31)

8. Jesus prayed that God would ___ ___ ___ ___
   (3 36)
   his disciples from the ___ ___ ___ ___ one.
   (38 11 34)

9. "The Father loves you because
   you ___ ___ ___ ___ me."
   (12 19 17)

10. "___ ___ ___ ___ ___ ___ ___ your Son
    (43 41 30)
    that the Son may bring glory to you."

Another Message

___ ___ ___ ___ ___ ___ ___ ___ ___ ___ ___ ___ ___
1 2 3 4 5 6 7 8 9 10 11 12 13

___ ___ ___ ___ ___ ___ ___ ___ ___ ___
14 15 16 17 18 19 20 21 22 23

___ ___ ___ ___ ___ ___ ___ ___ ___ ___ ___
24 25 26 27 28 29 30 31 32 33 34

___ ___ ___ ___ ___ ___ ___ ___ ___ ___ ___ ___ ___
35 36 37 38 39 40 41 42 43 44 45 46 47

Dial a Message

To find what eternal life is use the telephone dial numbers and letters as a key. The first number listed is the number on the dial; the second number is the letter.
For example: 23=c; 83=v.

__ __ __ __   __ __   __ __ __ __ __ __ __
81 42 43 73   43 73   32 81 32 72 62 21 53

__ __ __ __   __ __   __ __ __ __   __ __ __,
53 43 33 32   81 63   52 62 63 91   93 63 82

__ __ __   __ __ __   __ __ __ __   __ __ __,
81 42 32   63 62 32   81 72 82 32   41 63 31

__ __ __   __ __ __ __ __   __ __ __ __ __ __
21 62 31   51 32 73 82 73   23 42 72 43 73 81

__ __ __ __   __ __ __   __ __ __ __.
91 42 63 61   93 63 82   73 32 62 81

Prayer Requests

Below are prayer requests made by Jesus.

Using the story as a guide, put a check (√) in front of the requests Jesus made.

____ 1. I want my disciples to be with me.
____ 2. Don't take them out of the world.
____ 3. Glorify the Son that the Son may give glory to you.
____ 4. Make them (disciples) holy.
____ 5. Protect them from the evil one.
____ 6. I pray also for those who will believe in me through the message of the disciples.
____ 7. Protect the disciples from their enemies.
____ 8. Keep the disciples from quarreling among themselves.
____ 9. Help them to be servants to each other.

Write Your Own Prayer

Use the helps below to write your own prayer.

1. Confession
"Lord, I'm sorry for
a.
b.

2. Praise and Thanksgiving
"Lord, I praise you for
a.
b.
c.
"Lord, I'm thankful for
a.
b.

3. Intercession
List prayer requests you have for several other people.
a.
b.
c.

4. Petition
List several things you want to ask God for.
a.
b.
c.

"Hear my prayer, O Lord."

Group Activity 2

1. Keep a prayer chart of when you ask God for something specific, what you ask for, and when your prayer is answered.
2. Share occasions when God has answered specific prayers for you or your family.
3. Read together the Lord's Prayer (Matthew 6:9-13). What different kinds of prayer did Jesus use in this prayer?

13

Jesus Is Arrested

Group Activity 1

Matthew 26; Mark 14; Luke 22; John 18

Match the beginnings of the sentences on the left with the correct endings on the right by putting the letter on the space in front of the number.

BEGINNINGS

____ 1. Jesus knew that with God
____ 2. After the Passover meal the disciples and Jesus sang some hymns
____ 3. Jesus said to the police and soldiers
____ 4. When they had arrested Jesus and taken him away
____ 5. Jesus told the disciples to stay there
____ 6. During the confusion with the police and soldiers
____ 7. They went to a garden called Gethsemane
____ 8. Judas Iscariot arrived in the garden
____ 9. Jesus admonished the three disciples to stay awake
____ 10. Jesus healed the man's ear, saying to his disciples
____ 11. Peter, James, and John were asked to
____ 12. An angel of God appeared
____ 13. After praying awhile Jesus told the disciples
____ 14. Jesus prayed that the cup
____ 15. Peter, James, and John were so sleepy
____ 16. Jesus told the disciples that if he asked, God would send angels to help him but
____ 17. Jesus walked farther away taking

ENDINGS

E. and went out into the streets of Jerusalem together
A. where Jesus often went to pray
E. and pray so they would not fall into temptation
W. Peter, James, and John with him
T. watch with Jesus because he was so full of grief
A. of suffering would be taken from him
I. everything is possible
S. that they couldn't do as Jesus asked them
R. to pray that they wouldn't be put to the test
K. to strengthen Jesus as he prayed alone in the Garden.
H. the time has come for the Son of Man to be handed over to sinners
I. with the Roman soldiers and temple police
D. "Do what you're here for"
Y. Peter cut off the right ear of Malchus a servant of the high priest
S. "Everyone who takes up the sword will die by the sword"
T. that he must let this happen so the Scriptures would be fulfilled
B. his disciples ran away, scattered in every direction like sheep without a shepherd

Three Times

Jesus went away from his disciples to pray three times. Each time he prayed the same prayer. To discover Jesus' prayer, work the math puzzle to find the code.

A=9–1=_____ D=1+1=_____ G=0+6=_____ J=9+3=_____ M=5+5=_____ P=20+5=_____ S=6×3=_____ V=20–5=_____ Y=5–2=_____

B=10+3=_____ E=4-3=_____ H=10–3=_____ K=7–7=_____ N=25–2=_____ Q=9+8=_____ T=7×2=_____ W=2×8=_____ Z=3×8=_____

C=14–9=_____ F=20+7=_____ I=7×3=_____ L=15–6=_____ O=15+5=_____ R=20–1=_____ U=2+2=_____ X=12–1=_____

"14 8 0 1   14 7 21 18   5 4 25   30 27   18 4 27 27 1 19 21 23 6   8 16 8 3

27 19 30 10   10 1;   3 1 14   23 30 14   16 7 8 14   21   16 8 23 14,   13 4 14

16 7 8 14   3 30 4   16 8 23 14."

Encouragement for Discouragement

Use the number code from Three Times to find a verse to remember when you become discouraged.

9 1 8 15 1   8 9 9   3 30 4 19

16 30 19 19 21 1 18   16 21 14 7

7 21 10   [6 30 2]   13 1 5 8 4 18 1

7 1   5 8 19 1 18   27 30 19

3 30 4.   1 Peter 5:7

When You Feel Down

Jesus probably felt quite discouraged when his friends left him when he needed them. What do you do when you feel discouraged? What makes you discouraged? Finish the prayer.

Lord, sometimes I feel discouraged when

____

____

Help me to remember, Lord, that

____

____

Group Activity 2

Choose a friend and together write a definition of a friend. Share your ideas with the group.

14

Jesus Is Condemned and Denied

Group Activity 1

Matthew 26—27; Mark 14—15; Luke 22; John 18

Decide which six events from the story are most important. Illustrate them in the boxes. Write a short caption for each one.

Who Had Courage?

When Jesus was arrested and taken away his disciples lacked courage and they all ran away. But the Bible tells of others who were courageous and helped God in his work. To find who they were unscramble the names below, match them with the courageous act they did, and then put the names in the crossword puzzle.

Cascezahu ________	obeyed God when he was told to offer his only son as a sacrifice.
Thesar ________	refused to stop praying to God and was thrown into the lions' den
Bahmara ________	faced a giant with only a slingshot and trust in God
Vaddi ________	promised to give back what he had taken from the poor
Ladeni ________	had a plan to save her baby boy from the Pharaoh
Hebjecod ________	asked the king to save her Jewish people from death

How Is Your Courage?

Do you have courage to stand up for Jesus and what is right? What would you do in these situations?

- When you go to the library after school you discover the final exam for English lying on the table by the copy machine. You really need a good grade on the final because you did poorly on the midterm test. Should you look at the final? Should you take it to the office? What should you do?
- Some of the older boys on your street make fun and laugh at you because you go to Bible Club instead of play baseball. What should you do?
- You've been asked to join a special club at school—one which many popular kids join—but the initiation is to steal a candy bar from the school snack shop. What should you do?

Group Activity 2

How did you answer the situations in "How Is Your Courage?" Deuteronomy 31:8 gives good advice when you face situations in which you need courage. Read and memorize the verse.

Deuteronomy 31:8

The Lord himself will lead you
and be with you.
He will not fail you or abandon you,
so do not lose courage or be afraid.

15

The King of the Jews

Group Activity 1

Matthew 27; Mark 15; Luke 23; John 19; Acts 1

Put the events of the story in the correct order on the time line by placing the appropriate letters above the notches.

A—Pilate told the chief priests he couldn't find any reason to accuse Jesus.
B—Jesus refused to answer Herod's questions, so he was sent back to Pilate.
C—The council and the high priest took Jesus to Pilate, the governor.
D—Pilate questioned Jesus about being king of the Jews.
E—When Pilate discovered that Jesus was from Galilee he sent him to Herod Antipas, ruler of Galilee.
F—The chief priests used the thirty pieces of silver to buy a field to be used as a cemetery for foreigners.
G—Judas was sorry for what he had done.
H—Judas tried to give back the money to the chief priests and elders.
I—Jesus told Pilate his kingdom did not belong to this world.
J—Judas hanged himself.

___ /	___ /	___ /	___ /	___ /	___ /	___ /	___ /	___ /	___
1	2	3	4	5	6	7	8	9	10

Make a Sentence

Each group of words is part of a sentence—a beginning, a middle, and an end. Number the parts to make a sentence.

A. __ an innocent man
__ I have sinned because
__ I have betrayed

B. __ coins down in the
__ temple and left
__ Judas threw the

C. __ It is against the law
__ because it is blood money
__ to put this in the treasury

D. __ trial according to their own law
__ Pilate tried to get the
__ religious leaders to put Jesus on

E. __ fighting to save me
__ If my kingdom belonged to this
__ world my subjects would be

F. __ Herod sent Jesus
__ he was worthless
__ away saying that

Good Advice

While Jesus was being mistreated and questioned by his enemies he showed how he wanted his followers to treat those who mistreat them. Earlier he had tried to teach this to his disciples. Hidden in each line is a word. Find and circle the words to find a verse to remember when you are mistreated.

1. aczdlovejkmodpe
2. yourtsackdespng
3. bdeqsrhkenemies
4. amdijandcmuevjg
5. whalpsmntprayly
6. abfordmfrtjkzec
7. mthosedtkbisepn
8. blokcproqwhovwu
9. neclcpersecutee
10. youcamwtiyupeia

____

____

____

For You to Think About

It's hard to always show love, but Jesus will help you if you ask. Think about the following incidents and decide how you could show love in each situation.

- You have been waiting patiently for your turn when someone comes and rudely pushes you out of line and steps in your place. What will you do?
- Because you wear glasses some of the kids make fun of you and call you "four eyes."
- Some of your teammates make unkind remarks to you because you made a mistake and lost the ball game.
- Your little brother breaks your favorite model car after you have repeatedly asked him not to play with them.

Love Is the Winner

Jesus taught by word and example that his followers should show love to those who are not so easy to love. Draw a picture or describe a time when you showed love as Jesus taught. Or perhaps you remember a time when you didn't show love and you wish you would have.

Group Activity 2

1. Read the story of David and Saul in 1 Samuel 23—24. David showed love to Saul. Think of other examples of love in the Bible.
2. Make a collage of pictures showing love in action.
3. Read Luke 6:31. This verse also tells how to treat others. What does it mean?

16

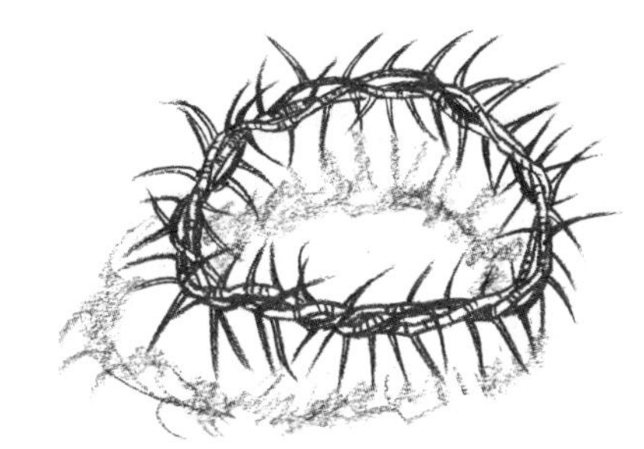

The Crown of Thorns

Group Activity 1

Matthew 27; Mark 15; Luke 23

In the activity below are the answers. Decide which is the best *question* to the *answer* given. Circle your choice.

1. Because they were jealous.
   a. Why did the priests take Jesus to Pilate?
   b. Why did the disciples leave Jesus?
   c. Why did the chief priests want Jesus killed?
2. "Not this man; we want Barabbas."
   a. When Pilate took Jesus outside his palace, what did the crowd say?
   b. What did the disciples say to the chief priests?
   c. What did Pilate's wife say to him?
3. Because he pretended to be the Son of God.
   a. Why was Pilate afraid to do what he thought was right?
   b. According to the law, why did the priests say Jesus must die?
   c. Why was the crowd shouting for Barabbas?
4. "I'll have him punished and let go."
   a. What did Herod say to Pilate?
   b. What did the crowd tell Pilate to do with Jesus?
   c. What did Pilate report to the chief priests?
5. They slapped his face and beat him with a stick.
   a. What did the crowds do to Barabbas?
   b. What did the soldiers do to punish Jesus?
   c. What did the disciples do to Pilate?
6. Jesus wouldn't answer.
   a. What did Jesus say to the disciples?
   b. What did Jesus say when the soldiers beat him?
   c. When Pilate asked Jesus where he came from what did he say?
7. "Have nothing to do with this innocent man."
   a. What message did the disciples give to Pilate?
   b. What did the crowd say to Pilate?
   c. What message did Pilate's wife send to him?
8. He washed his hands in a bowl of water right there in front of them.
   a. How did Pilate show the crowd his innocence?
   b. How did Jesus show Pilate that he was God's son?
   c. What did one of the disciples do to show his love for Jesus?
9. A crown of thorns and a purple robe.
   a. What were the priests wearing who went to see Pilate?
   b. What did Pilate's wife say that she wanted?
   c. What was Jesus wearing when he was presented to the crowd?
10. "Crucify him."
    a. What did the crowd shout to the disciples?
    b. When Pilate asked what he should do with Jesus, what did the crowd say?
    c. What did Barabbas say to the crowd?

Who Said It?

Match what was said with who said it by writing the correct name of the person on the line.

Pilate	crowd	chief priests
Jesus	Pilate's wife	soldiers

__________ "You have no power at all against me."

__________ "All hail! King of the Jews!"

__________ "Crucify him! Crucify him!"

__________ "If you set him free you're no friend of Caesar."

__________ "I've questioned him and don't find him guilty of any crime."

__________ "I've been upset all day about a dream I had about this man."

__________ "Look! See the man!"

__________ "Where do you come from?"

__________ "What should I do with this Jesus?"

__________ "Don't have anything to do with this man."

__________ "We want Barabbas!"

__________ "He must die because he pretended to be Son of God."

Which Way?

Think about the situations and decide what you would do.

1. There is a person in your class who gets on everyone's nerves and therefore is not included in any social activities. You know you should invite this person to your party but your other friends don't want you to because they say this person will ruin the party.
2. Some of your friends are saying how great a certain movie is. You really want to see it but it's rated "R," so your parents say you can't go. You've been invited to a friend's house and the plans for the evening include going to this movie. Should you go?

Spineless Pilate

Read the message about Pilate. You must decide where to start. Write down every third word until you have used all the words.

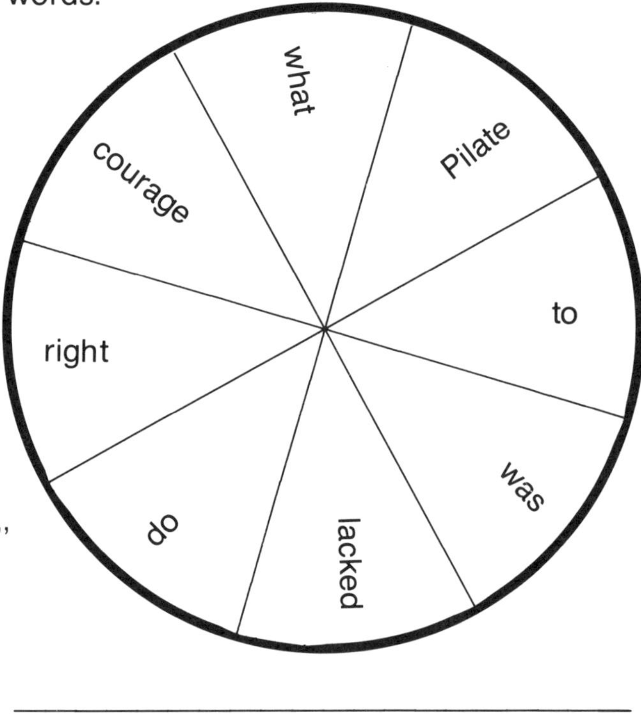

____

____

____

A Verse to Remember

Proverbs 3:6

Remember the Lord
in everything you do,
and he will show you
the right way.

Group Activity 2

Discuss your answers to "Which Way?"

17

The Lamb of God

Group Activity 1

Matthew 27; Mark 15; Luke 23; John 19

Six times Jesus spoke as he was hanging on the cross. Use A=1; B=2; to read what Jesus said each time.

1. 6 1 20 8 5 18,   6 15 18 7 9 22 5
   20 8 5 13   6 15 18   20 8 5 25
   4 15 14 ' 20   11 14 15 23   23 8 1 20
   20 8 5 25 ' 18 5   4 15 9 14 7.

2. 9   16 18 15 13 9 19 5   25 15 21,
   20 15 4 1 25   25 15 21 ' 12 12   2 5
   23 9 20 8   13 5   9 14
   16 1 18 1 4 9 19 5.

3. 23 15 13 1 14,   8 5 18 5   9 19
   25 15 21 18   19 15 14.   10 15 8 14,
   8 5 18 5   9 19   25 15 21 18
   13 15 20 8 5 18

4. 9   1 13   20 8 9 18 19 20 25.

5. 13 25   7 15 4!   13 25   7 15 4!
   23 8 25   8 1 22 5   25 15 21
   12 5 6 20   13 5?

6. 9 20   9 19   6 9 14 9 19 8 5 4!

Five Happenings

List five things that happened when Jesus died. Which event would have impressed you most if you had been there? Use words or a drawing on a separate paper to describe it.

1. ______________________________
2. ______________________________
3. ______________________________
4. ______________________________
5. ______________________________

Fill in the Blanks

Fill in the blanks then use the circled letters to finish the sentence.

1. _ _ _ (_) _ was forced to help Jesus carry his cross.
2. He was from _ (_) _ _ _ _, a town in (_) _ _ _ _ Africa.
3. Jesus was crucified at a place called _ _ (_) _ _ _ _ _.
4. The Latin name for the place of crucifixion was _ _ (_) _ _ _ _.
5. Jesus was crucified on the _ _ _ _ _ (_) cross.

Because Jesus knew his friends had left him and because he felt that God had left him, Jesus was a very

_ _ _ _ _ _ man.
3 1 2 5 4 2

Loneliness

Everyone gets lonely at times. Answer these questions.

I feel lonely when

____

____

When I feel lonely I

____

____

Names of God

There are many different names or descriptions of God in the Bible. Write the seven names of God listed here in the crossword. As you write each one decide why that name was given to God.

DEFENDER	PROTECTOR	SHEPHERD
MOTHER HEN	HOME	KING
	SHIELD	

Group Activity 2

1. What is God like? Share your ideas for each of God's names in "Names of God" or your drawing from "Five Happenings."
2. Think of something in your world that shows how God comforts the lonely. How does God comfort you?
3. What do you think are the saddest words in this story? Why?

18

In the Tomb

Group Activity 1

Matthew 27; Mark 15; Luke 23; John 19

Number the events of the story in the order in which they happened.

__ Joseph and Nicodemus wrapped the body of Jesus in a linen shroud.

__ The soldiers broke the legs of the robbers who were crucified with Jesus.

__ When the sun went down it was the Sabbath and all rested as the Sabbath law required.

__ The women from Galilee watched as the men prepared Jesus' body for burial.

__ The soldiers guarded the tomb and sealed the stone to make sure no one would steal Jesus' body.

__ A soldier pierced Jesus' side with a spear.

__ Because it was almost Sabbath the Jewish leaders requested that the legs of the prisoners be broken to hurry the executions.

__ Joseph went to Pilate to ask for Jesus' body so he could bury him.

__ Jesus was buried in a stone tomb in a garden close to Calvary.

__ On the Sabbath the Pharisees and chief priests asked Pilate to put a guard at the tomb so Jesus' friends would not steal the body.

Map Study

Turn to the map of Jerusalem, page 6. Then follow the directions below carefully. If you need help, check the Bible references or the story.

1. Put a red X beside the Garden of Gethsemane. Briefly write two events that happened here. Mark 14:32-42; Luke 22:47-52
2. Draw a green circle around the high priest's palace. What two events happened here? Luke 22:54-60; Mark 14:60
3. Look up Mark 14:14-25. What happened? Find that location on the map and circle it in blue.
4. Locate the palace of the Roman governor. Draw an orange line under it. What happened to Jesus here? Matthew 27:1-2; Mark 15:16-20
5. Circle the Hill of Calvary whatever color you choose. Let the color describe your feelings about what happened to Jesus at this spot. Draw three crosses there.

A Character Sketch

Because of his actions Joseph of Arimathea will always be remembered. Look in the story and find four things about this Joseph. Look up John 19:38 to find one other characteristic of Joseph.

Joseph was 1) ____________________

2) ____________________

3) ____________________

4) ____________________

5) ____________________

(Matthew 27:57; Mark 15:43; Luke 23:51; John 19:38)

What Is Love?

1 John 3:16 describes love. Follow the directions to discover an answer to the question. Follow the number 1 until you form a word. Do the same for each number until you have the entire verse.

5 20 8 1 17 10 7 15 12 24 6 19
K O I T O G L E L B W G

23 9 24 21 8 22 19 24 3 10 21 13
O C R L S F I O H A I F

21 1 17 6 24 9 12 18 5 21 14 19
V H U H T H I T N E U V

20 10 6 12 9 14 1 16 17 20 9 6
U V A F R S I T G R I T

18 11 5 16 3 16 7 13 4 24 1 22
O H O O O O O O W H S O

12 2 21 7 9 24 10 23 13 5 9 19
E I S V S E E U R W T E

22 4 17 11 24 3 24 23 7 17 2 11
R E H I R W S R E T S S

____ __ ___ __

____ ____ ____

__: _____ ______ ____

___ ____ ___ __.

W__ ___ _____ __

____ ___ _______

___ ___ _________!

Love in Action

Love can be shown and described in many different ways. In the letters find five words that describe love or ways to show love. Then use the words to write Jesus a love note in the heart telling him how you will show love.

pothsharetwelmo
givetatelpzxprk
biwelcomeobltmo
forgivetzesocti
ctilpecaremnelp

Group Activity 2

1. Show your love to Jesus by making bookmarks for an older friend in your church or neighborhood. Cut a piece of stiff paper 2″ × 6″. Use stickers or draw a picture to decorate the bookmark. Write a message or a favorite verse on it.
2. Study the illustration on page 92 of "God's Suffering Servant." What does it tell you? Imagine yourself in the picture. Describe your feelings.

19

The Empty Tomb

Group Activity 1

Matthew 28; Mark 16; Luke 24; John 20

Answer these questions about the story.

1. On the first day of the week some of the women went to _ _ _ _ _ (17 1 7 1 6) the tomb.
2. They brought _ _ _ _ _ _ (7 19 1 10 5 7) to anoint the body, according to the Jewish custom.
3. As they walked along they were wondering who would roll away the _ _ _ _ (11 13 4 5) stone from the entrance.
4. When the women saw that the stone was rolled away, and saw a young man sitting in the tomb they were _ _ _ _ _ _ _ _ _ (6 5 8 8 1 2 1 5 20).
5. The young man told the women "Jesus isn't there for he has _ _ _ _ _ (8 1 7 5 14).
6. The young man told the women to tell the disciples that Jesus would meet them in _ _ _ _ _ _ _ (4 15 16 1 16 5 5).
7. The disciples said "_ _ _ _ _ _ _ _ (14 9 14 7 5 14 7 5)" when the women told them that Jesus was alive.
8. Even so Peter and _ _ _ _ (18 9 11 14) decided to go to the tomb to see for themselves if what the women said was true.
9. When they saw the empty tomb and the linen clothes used to wrap the body, they _ _ _ _ _ _ _ _ (3 5 16 1 5 17 5 20).
10. The next person to visit the empty tomb was Mary _ _ _ _ _ _ _ _ _ (21 15 4 20 15 16 5 14 5).
11. When Mary looked into the tomb she saw two _ _ _ _ _ _ (15 14 4 5 16 7) sitting where Jesus had been.
12. When she recognized him, Jesus greeted Mary with the words, "_ _ _ _ _ (19 5 15 10 5). be with you."
13. Mary fell in front of Jesus to _ _ _ _ _ _ _ (12 9 8 7 11 1 19) him.
14. Jesus told Mary to tell his disciples that he was going up to his _ _ _ _ _ _ (2 15 6 11 5 8).

Read a Message

Use the letters above the numbers in Group Activity 1 to find an important message about the story.

_ _ _ _ _ _ _   _ _ _ _ _   _ _ _ _ _   _ _   _ _ _
3 5 10 15 13 7 5   18 5 7 13 7   16 1 17 5 7   12 5   10 15 14

_ _ _ _ _ _ _   _ _ _   _ _ _ _   _ _   _ _ _ _ _ _ _   _ _ _ _!
8 5 10 5 1 17 5   11 1 7   4 1 2 6   9 2   5 6 5 8 14 15 16   16 1 2 5

Jesus Is Lord

Lord is used for someone who has power, respect, and authority. What kind of Lord is Jesus? He makes demands and promises. After filling this chart you will have a better idea of Jesus as Lord.

	Promise (what Jesus will do)	Demand (what you must do)
Matthew 11:28-30		
John 15:9-10, 12		
John 3:16		
John 14:23		
1 John 5:14-15		

Group Activity 2

1. Discuss the "Jesus Is Lord" chart. What demands and promises does Jesus make? What kind of Lord is he?
2. Together make an Easter banner or poster using the words JESUS IS RISEN or HALLELUJAH! JESUS LIVES.

20

Jesus Appears to His Disciples

Group Activity 1

Mark 16; Luke 24

Circle the letter (or letters) in front of the correct answer.

1. How many of Jesus' followers were traveling together?
   a. four
   b. twelve
   c. two
   d. none of the above
2. These friends were traveling to a village called
   a. Emmaus
   b. Jerusalem
   c. Bethany
   d. none of the above
3. Their topic of conversation was
   a. the bad weather
   b. the earthquake on Friday
   c. about all the events that had taken place in Jerusalem
   d. none of the above
4. As they walked along another person joined them. Who was this person?
   a. Abraham
   b. John the Baptist
   c. Pilate
   d. none of the above
5. What did the stranger ask the friends?
   a. "What's all this you are talking about?"
   b. "Why are you so sad and gloomy?"
   c. Where are you going?"
6. What did Cleopas answer?
   a. He told him about Jesus and what had happened in Jerusalem the previous days.
   b. He told him about the fights and quarrels the disciples were having.
   c. He shared their hopes for Jesus.
7. What hope did they have for Jesus?
   a. That he would make everyone well
   b. That he would set Israel free
   c. That he would come down from the cross.
8. What were these disciples excited about?
   a. The news that the Roman soldiers were leaving their country.
   b. The reports of the angels that Jesus was alive.
   c. The reports of the empty tomb.
9. What did this stranger help these disciples understand?
   a. He explained the Old testament Scriptures and why Jesus came.
   b. He explained why the weather was acting so strangely.
   c. He explained why they needed to suffer as they did.
10. What happened when the stranger gave the bread to the disciples?
    a. They recognized him as Jesus.
    b. They ate the bread and continued their conversation.
    c. Jesus vanished from their sight.
11. What did these two friends do as soon as Jesus vanished?
    a. Searched the Scriptures to see if what Jesus had told them was true.
    b. Immediately returned to Jerusalem.
    c. Told the eleven disciples what had happened to them.
12. What news did the eleven disciples have to share with Cleopas and his friend?
    a. "It's true! The Lord has arisen. He appeared to Peter!"
    b. "We have found the body."
    c. "We have seen Jesus."

What If...

We know Jesus is with us, even though we can't see him. But suppose suddenly you *could* see Jesus walking with you down the street or riding beside you in the school bus. What questions would you like to ask him about the last several days of his life? Write one question. ____________________

____

____

What question would you like to ask him about life today? ______________

____

____

A Verse to Remember

The Bible teaches what Jesus is like. The Bible, God's Word, also guides us. Circle the first letter and then circle every third letter. Put the verse you find on a card, decorate it, and put it at a place where you will see it often.

Y A B O C D U C E R I L W W C O
E F R K J D M I I A Z S B P A A
L L Z Q A A M M A C P D F T G E
O L M G P O U J L I A C D E P E
E M M A G E H P A M N N E N D C
Q A R S L O V I W X G A Z H T E
T B D F R O O L A R E S M R Q Y
W P P E I A C E T S H H. O M P N
T S T R A B D L J K M T E.
119:105

____

____

____

____

Why?

Jesus' friends on the way to Emmaus needed Jesus to explain to them why he came and why events happened as they did. Use the consonants listed to complete the words by the cross to find why Jesus came. Cross out each letter as you use it. Color the cross.

R F C F G
H J L M S
S S T V S

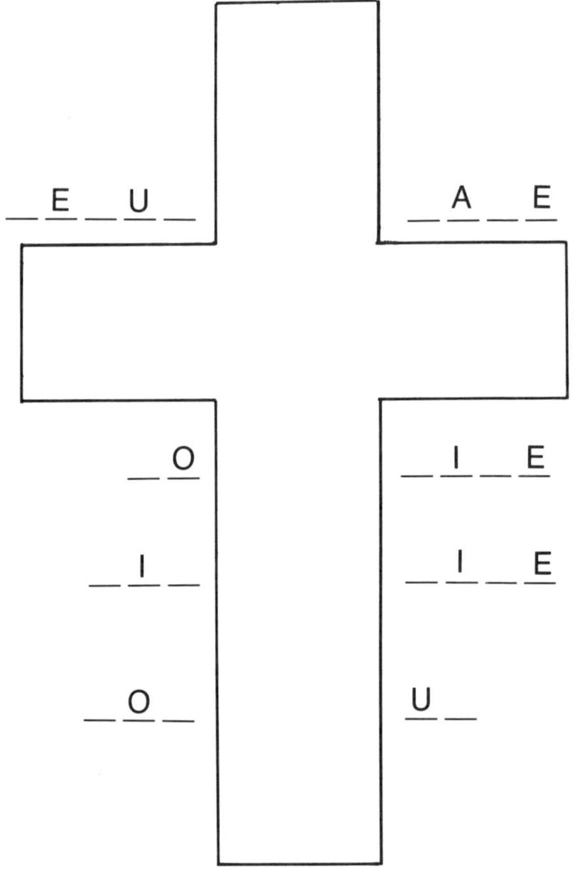

Group Activity 2

1. The disciples in the story did not recognize Jesus until he broke bread for them. How do you recognize Jesus? How does he make himself known to you?
2. Tell your favorite Bible story about Jesus.
3. Play a game. Have the teacher or another student call out a Bible reference. See who can locate the reference first and call out the last word of the verse.

21

"Blessed Are Those Who Believe"

Group Activity 1

Luke 24; John 20

1. Jesus told his disciples to wait in (5 across) for power to come from heaven.
2. When Jesus appeared to the disciples they were filled with (2 across).
3. The disciples kept the doors of their meeting room locked because they were (6 down) of the religious leaders.
4. Jesus asked for something to eat; the disciples gave him some cooked (12 down).
5. Jesus said to his disciples, "(13 down) be with you."
6. Jesus' disciples thought he was a (4 down).
7. (8 down) was the disciple who was absent and refused to believe Jesus was alive.
8. Jesus told the disciples, "Look! Ghosts don't have (10 across) and (17 down).
9. Jesus opened the minds of the disciples so they could understand the (7 across).
10. When the disciples realized that Jesus was alive, they were filled with (15 down).
11. Jesus told his disciples they were to be (14 across) to what they had seen and heard.
12. Jesus breathed on his disciples to give them the (11 down) (two words).
13. Jesus told Thomas to stop being a (16 across) and become a (9 down).
14. In explaining the Scriptures, Jesus told his disciples that the (3 across) must suffer, die, and on the third day rise from the dead.
15. The (18 across) of God's (1 down) of sins must be preached to everyone.

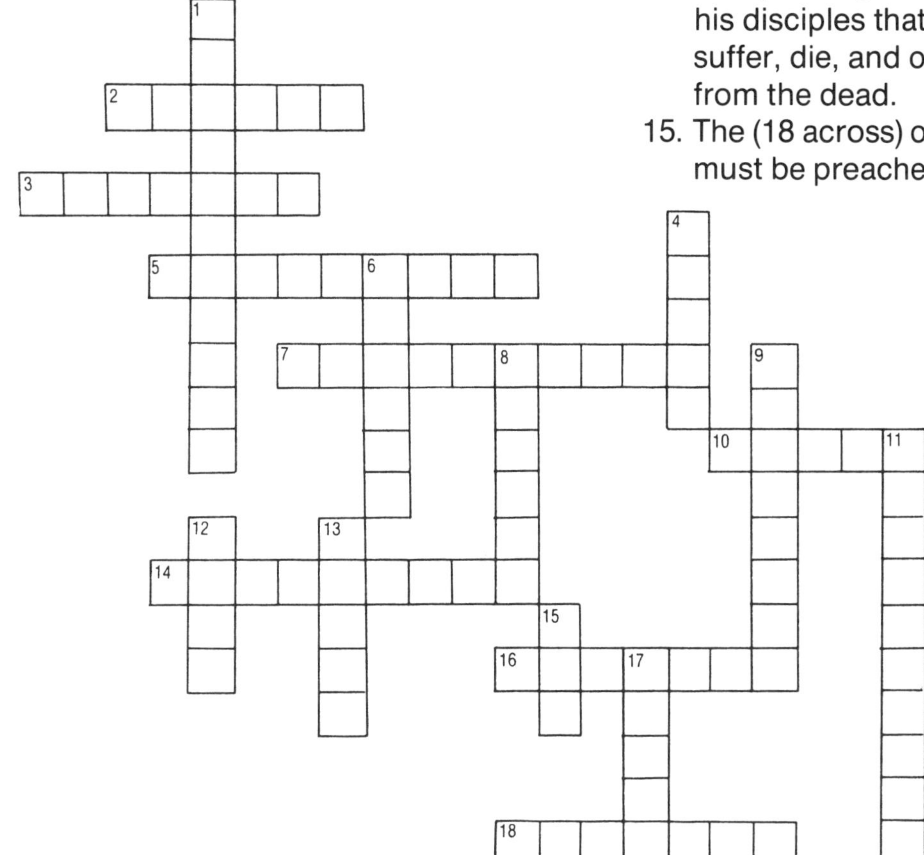

The Holy Spirit

Jesus gave his disciples the Holy Spirit. Look up the verses to find out more about the Holy Spirit. In each box write a few words of description of what the Holy Spirit does.

John 14:16
2 Corinthians 3:6b
John 14:26
Acts 1:8
John 16:13
Romans 8:16
Romans 8:14

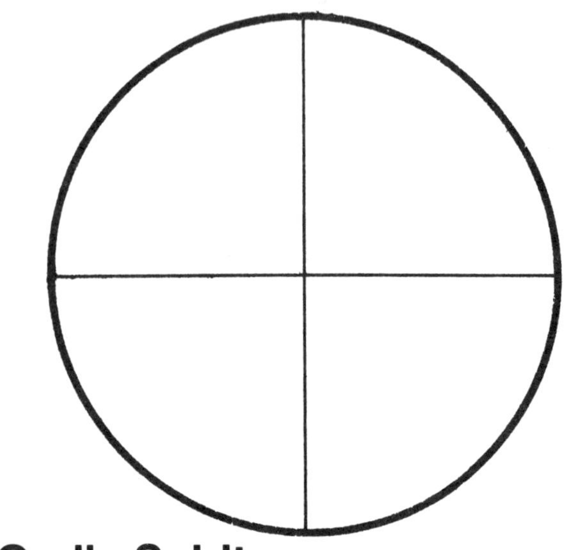

God's Spirit

Learn four facts about God's Spirit. Unscramble each fact and write it in one section of the circle.

G A H C E S N O Y U
S I W P F L U R O E
S A A Y L W H I T W U O Y
P L E H S U Y O K W R O

Dial a Verse

To find what Jesus said about the Holy Spirit, you, power, and witnessing, use the telephone dial numbers and letters as a key. The first number listed is the number on the dial; the second number is the letter. For example 42=H; 73=S.

22 82 81 91 42 32 62 81 42 32 42 63 53 93

73 71 43 72 43 81 23 63 61 32 73

82 71 63 62 93 63 82, 93 63 82 91 43 81 42

22 32 33 43 53 53 32 31 91 43 53 53

71 63 91 32 72 21 62 31 93 63 82

91 43 53 53 22 32

91 43 81 62 32 73 73 32 73 33 63 72

61 32 43 62 51 32 72 82 73 21 53 32 61.

43 62 21 53 53 51 82 31 32 21 21 62 31

73 21 61 21 72 43 21. 21 62 31 81 63

81 42 32 32 62 31 73 63 33 81 42 32

32 21 72 81 42. 21 23 81 73 1:8

Group Activity 2

1. Discuss the statement Jesus made when he said, "Happy are those who believe without seeing me!" John 20:29

22

"Feed My Lambs"

Group Activity 1

John 21

Put a ☺ in front of all the things that Jesus did in the story.

____ 1. Jesus told his disciples that he was disappointed in them because they had run away when he needed them.

____ 2. Three times Jesus asked Peter if he (Peter) loved Jesus.

____ 3. Jesus also asked John if he loved Jesus.

____ 4. Jesus performed miracles for the disciples so they would believe.

____ 5. Jesus acted surprised that his friends did not recognize him.

____ 6. Jesus prepared breakfast for the disciples who had fished all night.

____ 7. Jesus told the disciples that he would soon leave them.

____ 8. Jesus told the disciples to put their nets on the other side of the boat.

____ 9. Jesus told his disciples to go to the Garden of Gethsemane to wait for him.

____ 10. Jesus told Peter, "Follow me; don't be concerned about John."

____ 11. After breakfast Jesus asked the disciples to take him for a boat ride around the lake.

Right or Wrong?

Read each pair of sentences. Decide which one is correct. Circle the letter in front of the correct sentence. In some cases both sentences may be either correct or neither sentence may be correct.

1. a. Because Peter had denied Jesus three times, Jesus gave Peter the opportunity to say he loved Jesus three times.
   b. Jesus asked Peter the same questions three times to show Peter that he was mad at him.
2. a. Jesus told Peter to take care of his animals.
   b. Jesus told Peter to look after his followers.
3. a. Jesus wanted to show Peter and the other disciples that he had forgiven Peter for denying him.
   b. Jesus wanted to show Peter and the others that Peter had special work to do for Jesus.
4. a. Peter acted like he did not want to help Jesus with this special work.
   b. Peter wanted to know how he could help Jesus.
5. a. Jesus performed a miracle to help his disciples know who he was.
   b. Jesus told his disciples who he was.
6. a. Because they probably were unsure of what to do next, Peter and the other disciples who had been fishermen went fishing.
   b. Because they were afraid, Peter and some of the disciples took a long boat ride to a faraway place so Jesus could not find them.

Faithful Followers

How many of these people of faith do you know? Use the names from the list.

a. Nicodemus	g. Moses	m. Esther
b. Elizabeth	h. Abraham	n. Joseph
c. Stephen	i. Peter	o. Philip
d. Isaiah	j. Jacob	p. Samuel
e. Job	k. Elijah	q. Joshua
f. Thomas	l. Daniel	r. Simeon

__ 1. The disciple who would not believe Jesus was alive until he saw Jesus' wounds.
__ 2. The leader of the Israelites when they left Egypt.
__ 3. One of Jesus' disciples who told Nathanael about Jesus.
__ 4. He came after dark to ask questions of Jesus.
__ 5. Three times this disciple denied knowing Jesus.
__ 6. God told him to take the baby Jesus to Egypt.
__ 7. The mother of John the Baptist.
__ 8. He was told by God to leave his home country to go to another land.
__ 9. A great Old Testament prophet who told about Jesus' coming.
__ 10. The son of Isaac who dreamed about God and a ladder reaching to heaven.
__ 11. He had many trials and hardships but remained faithful even when his friends urged him to curse God.
__ 12. He became the leader of the Israelites after Moses died.
__ 13. She was queen of Persia who saved her Jewish people from destruction.
__ 14. This man was taken by a whirlwind into heaven.
__ 15. He was saved from the lions' den because of his faith.
__ 16. God promised him he would not die until he had seen the Messiah.
__ 17. He obeyed the Lord when the Lord called him in the temple.
__ 18. He was stoned because he preached about Jesus.

To Think About

Jesus helped Peter change from a man who was afraid to say he knew Jesus to a man who had courage to tell about Jesus. Jesus helped Peter forget past failures and look ahead. What are some ways in which God needs to help you change just as he helped Peter? Read the list and check those that you need help with. Add others. Be honest.

____Obey without arguing
____Stop complaining
____Always tell the truth
____Be honest
____Be more dependable
____Be kind to those you don't like
____Be on time
____Work harder
____Complete things you start

Code a Verse

At times you may fail. You may do something that you thought you had stopped doing. But Paul gives good advice when this happens. Find and read Philippians 3:13b—14. Use a number code and put this verse in code form for a friend to solve.

Group Activity 2

Peter was told to take care of Jesus' lambs, which meant, "Tell others about Jesus." Be specific and name ways you can feed Jesus' lambs.

23

Jesus Goes Up to Heaven

Group Activity 1

Matthew 28; Mark 16; Luke 24

Jesus gave his disciples instructions to do five things. Use the code to discover what Jesus wanted his disciples to do. Each letter on the outside of the circle stands for the letter below it on the inner circle.

1. R Z E Z L W W A L C E D Z Q E S P H Z C W O.

2. A C P L N S R Z Z O Y P H D Z Q R Z O'D C F W P.

3. X L V P O T D N T A W P D Z Q

   P G P C J Y L E T Z Y.

4. M L A E T K P Y P H

   O T D N T A W P D

5. E P L N S E S P X

   E Z Z M P J X J

   N Z X X L Y O X P Y E D.

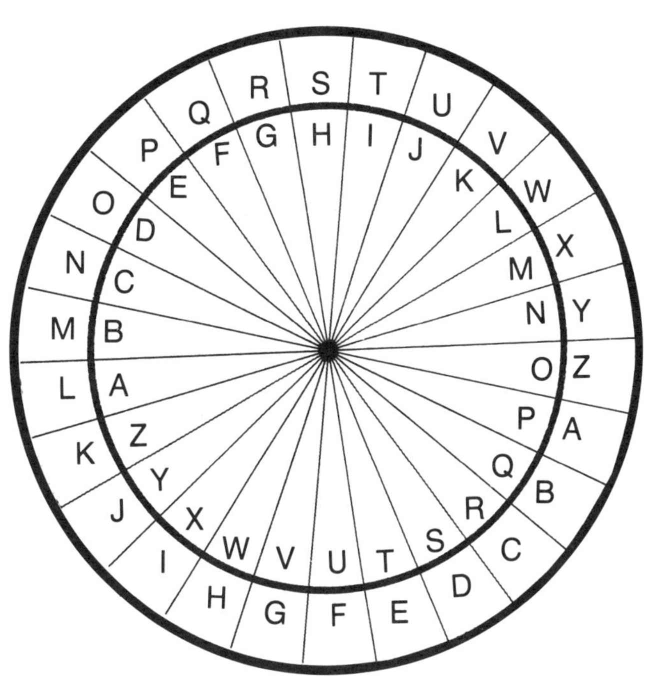

Who Am I?

How well do you remember events and people in the last week of Jesus' life? See if you can recall the answers without looking in the book.

__________ 1. I was released instead of Jesus.

__________ 2. I asked Jesus to remember me as we hung on the crosses.

__________ 3. I said, "Pull down this temple and in three days I will raise it up."

__________ 4. I poured expensive perfume on Jesus' feet while he was at supper.

__________ 5. I said, "You'll never wash my feet."

__________ 6. I betrayed Jesus for thirty pieces of silver.

__________ 7. "I am the way, the truth, and the life."

__________ 8. Jesus asked us to stay awake and pray with him in the Garden of Gethsemane but we didn't. (Three names)

__________ 9. I cut off the ear of Malchus when Jesus was arrested.

__________ 10. When Jesus was arrested we scattered like sheep without a shepherd and left Jesus alone.

__________ 11. Three times I said I didn't know Jesus.

__________ 12. I gave Jesus over to the chief priests to be crucified.

__________ 13. I told my husband to have nothing to do with Jesus because he was innocent.

__________ 14. Jesus appeared to me and I thought at first he was the gardener.

__________ 15. I was one of Jesus' followers who spoke with Jesus on the road to Emmaus.

__________ 16. I refused to believe Jesus was alive until I had seen him and touched his wounds.

__________ 17. Jesus asked me three times if I loved him.

__________ 18. I was a secret follower of Jesus who asked Pilate for Jesus' body to bury it in my tomb.

Jesus' Promise

Jesus made a promise to his disciples. It is a promise to you also. Use the same letter code as in Group Activity 1 to read Jesus' promise. Memorize the promise.

_ _ _ _ _ _ _ _   _   _ _

C P X P X M P C   T   L X

_ _ _ _   _ _ _   _ _ _ _ _ _,

H T E S   J Z F   L W H L J D

_ _ _ _ _   _ _ _   _ _ _

F Y E T W   E S P   P Y O

_ _   _ _ _ _.

Z Q   E T X P

Group Activity 2

Talk about the characters in "Who Am I?" Which character are you most like? Together describe a faithful follower of Jesus.

24

God Shows His Glory

Group Activity 1

John 1

Reread the story and fill in the chart. First answer the question.

Who did John, the writer of this passage

call the Word? _ _ _ _ _

Facts About the Word:
What Is the Word Like?

1. ______________________________
2. ______________________________
3. ______________________________
4. ______________________________
5. ______________________________

What Has He Done?

1. ______________________________
2. ______________________________
3. ______________________________
4. ______________________________
5. ______________________________
6. ______________________________
7. ______________________________

What's in It for You?

Because of the Word and what he has done, two things are helpful for you. Use the number code to discover these two benefits for you.

	2	4	6	8	0
1	A	B	C	D	E
3	F	G	H	I	J
5	K	L	M	N	O
7	P	R	S	T	U
9	V	W	X	Y	Z

1. _ _ _   _ _ _ _   _ _ _
98 50 70   36 12 92 10   78 36 10

_ _ _ _ _   _ _   _ _ _ _ _ _
72 50 94 10 74   78 50   14 10 16 50 56 10

_   _ _ _ _ _   _ _   _ _ _.
12   16 36 38 54 18   50 32   34 50 18

2. _ _ _   _ _ _   _ _ _ _
98 50 70   16 12 58   52 58 50 94

_ _ _ _   _ _ _   _ _   _ _ _ _.
94 36 12 78   34 50 18   38 76   54 38 52 10

Characteristics of God

One of Jesus' purposes on earth was to show what God is like. Circle all the phrases that show a characteristic of God.

Check the Bible references if you are unsure. First Corinthians 10:13; Acts 10:34; Nehemiah 9:17b; Psalms 7:11; 46:1; 1 John 4:8; Matthew 10:29-31.

easily angered *frustrated by our mistakes* *all knowing* *mean*
strength
righteous judge *easily upset*
love *makes fun of us* *wishy-washy* *slow to anger*
forgiving *gracious* *keeps promises* *cheats*
judges quickly
shelter *doesn't play favorites*

Search for a Message

Hiding in these words and numbers is a message. To find it follow the number one until you have found a word. Do the same for each number until you have the entire message. Write it on the lines.

C	U	G	T	L	W
2	5	7	3	9	6
S	J	I	A	S	H
4	1	9	2	5	6
E	O	M	H	S	K
1	7	2	4	1	9
O	D	E	U	A	I
4	7	9	1	6	8
E	T	S	W	O	S
2	6	8	4	3	1

_ _ _ _ _ (1)   _ _ _ _ (2)   _ _ (3)

_ _ _ _ (4)   _ _ (5)   _ _ _ _ (6)

_ _ _ (7)   _ _ (8)   _ _ _ _ (9).

Sonlight

You know what sunlight is, but what is Sonlight? Write an acrostic using the word Sonlight. Describe Sonlight. For help use these references: John 8:12; 12:35-36; 1 John 1:7.

S
O
N
L
I
G
H
T

Group Activity 2

1. How are light and Jesus similar?
2. As a class write a Sonlight acrostic using some of the individual ideas.

Answer Key

1

Group Activity 1

G / F / A / H / E /
1 2 3 4 5
I / B / D / J / C /
6 7 8 9 10

Expectations

1. Perhaps Jesus was the one the prophets had spoken about.
2. Perhaps he was the leader who would save them from their enemies.
3. Perhaps he would drive out the Romans and set up the kingdom of God.

God's Anointed One

1. Healed the sick.
2. Cast out demons.
3. Opened the eyes of the blind and the ears of the deaf.
4. Raised a man from the dead.

2

Group Activity 1

1. sheep
2. cattle
3. courtyard
4. angry
5. hideout
6. Father's
7. sign
8. Scriptures
9. temple
10. disciples

sacrifices

What Is Faith?

"To have faith is to be sure of the things we hope for, to be certain of the things we cannot see." Hebrews 11:1

3

Group Activity 1

1. C
2. C
3. B
4. H
5. G
6. C
7. A
8. C
9. D
10. A
11. F
12. A
13. E
14. A

Parables

mustard seed
yeast
growing seed
good seed and weeds

Angry Landlord

God's special gift to his people was Jesus.
No

Jesus' Message

Because you do not accept me, the kingdom of God will be given to someone who will produce fruit for the kingdom.

A Verse to Learn

I am the vine, and you are the branches. Whoever remains in me, and I in him, will bear much fruit; for you can do nothing without me.

4

Group Activity 1

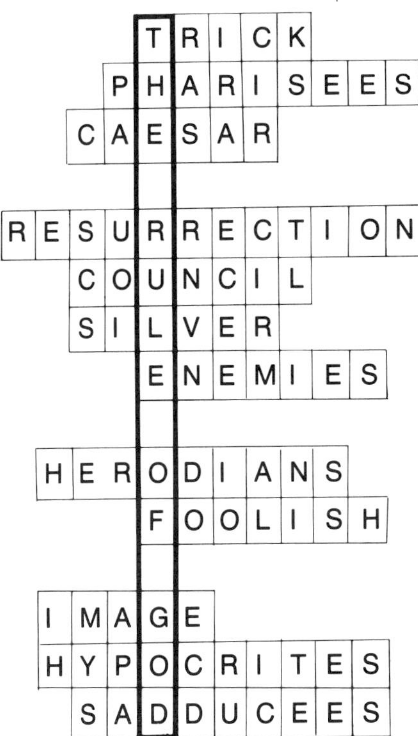

Important Words

The rule of God

A Verse to Remember

Everything you do or say, then, should be done in the name of the Lord Jesus.

5

Group Activity 1

1. T
2. F
3. T
4. F
5. F
6. T
7. T
8. T
9. F
10. F
11. T

Jesus' Warning

Watch out! Do not be a phony.

How to Become a Big Shot

H=7; M=3; E=6; S=4; T=1; R=2; O=5
To be the greatest, one must serve others.

A Verse to Remember

Create a pure heart in me, O God, and put a new and loyal spirit in me. Psalms 51:10

Group Activity 1

1. There will be wars.
2. There will be earthquakes.
3. There will be famines.
4. There will be terrifying signs from heaven.
5. Jesus' followers will be arrested.
6. There will be false prophets and false messiahs.
7. The sun and moon will not give light.
8. The stars will fall from the sky.

Jesus' Promises

1. Don't prepare speeches. Use the words I will give you through the Holy Spirit.
2. Everyone who stands firm to the end will be saved.

Group Activity 1

A Warning

"Watch out! Be prepared. You don't know the day or hour when the Son of Man will come."

Jesus the Model

Luke 6:36: "Be merciful just as your Father is merciful."

Group Activity 1

1. b
2. b, c
3. b, c
4. c

5. b, c
6. b, c
7. a, b, c
8. a, b

9. b, c
10. a
11. b
12. a

Costly But Worth It

Jesus was pleased with the woman who anointed him.

Recognition

1. She has done a beautiful thing for me.
2. What this woman did will be told and she will be remembered.

Group Activity 1

1. S
2. E
3. R
4. V
5. A
6. N
7. T
8. K
9. I
10. N
11. G

Who Me? A Servant?

Matthew 6:2-4	Help the needy
Matthew 6:16-18	Pray . . .
Matthew 5:21-22	Don't call . . .
Matthew 28:19-20	Tell . . .
Matthew 25:36a	Clothe . . .
Matthew 25:35b	Show . . .
Matthew 19:16-17	Keep . . .
Matthew 25:34-35a	Help feed . . .
Matthew 7:1	Don't judge
Matthew 25:36c	Visit . . .
Matthew 22:37, 40	Love . . .
Matthew 25:36b	Care . . .

Color It Out

"And look out for one another's interests, not just . . . your own."

Disciple Search

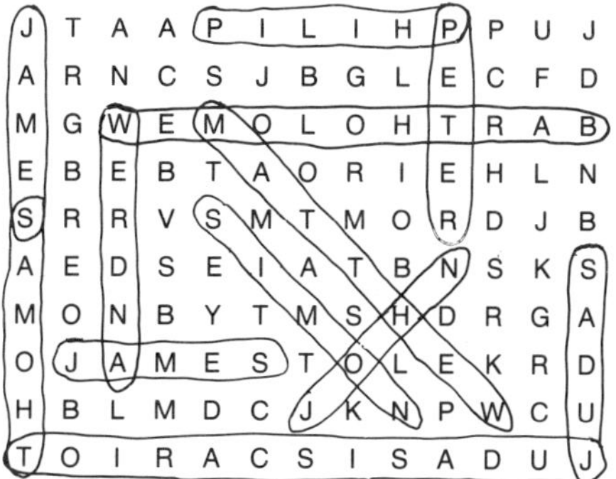

10

Group Activity 1

Answers for this activity appear in "Old Versus New" below

Old Versus New

T	H	E		B	L	O	O	D
1	2	3		4	5	6	7	8

O	F		J	E	S	U	S		I	S
9	10		11	12	13	14	15		16	17

A		S	Y	M	B	O	L		O	F
18		19	20	21	22	23	24		25	26

T	H	E		N	E	W
27	28	29		30	31	32

C	O	V	E	N	A	N	T
33	34	35	36	37	38	39	40

Explore a Maze

J	E	S	U	S	S	H	L	M	N	T	Q
P	O	P	L	S	A	O	G	M	Z	C	A
C	L	E	T	H	O	M	C	O	M	E	Z
E	P	T	L	O	S	A	S	T	T	A	R
L	E	A	P	W	E	P	M	I	T	G	J
F	J	D	T	E	F	S	I	A	T	A	N
O	U	E	L	D	A	A	A	N	I	L	P
P	M	N	O	U	N	E	K	W	J	A	M
T	P	Y	U	E	E	F	W	O	P	A	T
S	A	L	R	M	W	W	A	Y	L	A	E
K	J	U	D	A	S	J	Y	T	I	C	E
J	S	U	S	E	J	S	E	O	G	O	D

Jesus showed a new way to God.

11

Group Activity 1

1. I will go prepare a place for you.
2. I will come back for you.
3. You will have life because of me.
4. I will ask the Father to send the Holy Spirit to be your teacher.
5. I will give you my peace.
6. I will not leave you alone.

The Way to the Father

1. rooms
2. whoever
3. helper
4. truth
5. vine
6. fruit
7. gardener
8. trimmed
9. joy
10. world

I am the way, the truth, and the life.

Jesus Gives Hope

"Do not be worried and upset," Jesus told them. "You believe in God; believe also in me."

12

Group Activity 1

1. disciples
2. away
3. understand
4. sorrow joy
5. good guide
6. world brave
7. alone with
8. keep evil
9. love
10. glorify

Another Message

Ask and you will receive and your joy will be overflowing.

Dial a Message

This is eternal life: to know you, the one true God, and Jesus Christ whom you sent.

Prayer Requests

These need checks: 1, 2, 3, 4, 5, 6

13

Group Activity 1

1. I	10. S
2. E	11. T
3. D	12. K
4. B	13. H
5. E	14. A
6. Y	15. S
7. A	16. T
8. I	17. W
9. R	

Three Times

A=8	N=23
B=13	O=30
C=5	P=25
D=2	Q=17
E=1	R=19
F=27	S=18
G=6	T=14
H=7	U=4
I=21	V=15
J=12	W=16
K=0	X=11
L=9	Y=3
M=10	Z=24

Take this cup of suffering away from me; yet not what I want, but what you want.

Encouragement for Discouragement

Leave all your worries with him [God], because he cares for you.

14

Who Had Courage?

Zacchaeus,4
Esther, 6
Abraham, 1
Daniel, 2
David, 3
Jochebed, 5

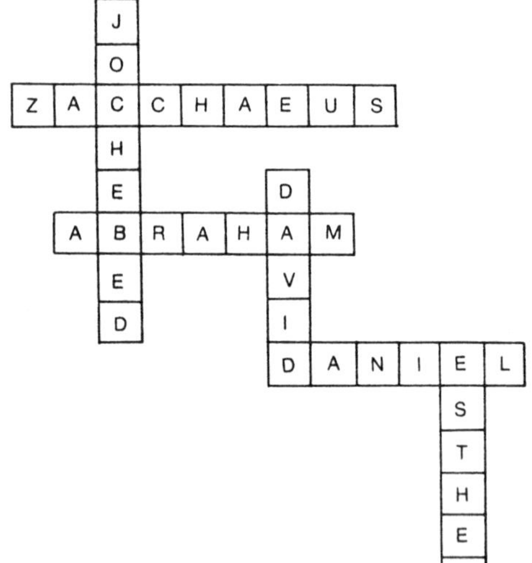

15

Group Activity 1

G / H / J / F / C / D /
1 2 3 4 5 6
I / A / E / B /
7 8 9 10

Make a Sentence

A. 3, 1, 2
B. 2, 3, 1
C. 1, 3, 2
D. 3, 1, 2
E. 3, 1, 2
F. 1, 3, 2

Good Advice

Love your enemies and pray for those who persecute you.

16

Group Activity 1

1. c.
2. a.
3. b.
4. c.
5. b.
6. c.
7. c.
8. a.
9. c.
10. b.

Who Said It?

Jesus
Soldiers
crowds
chief priests
Pilate
Pilate's wife
Pilate
Pilate
Pilate
Pilate's wife
crowd
chief priests

Spineless Pilate

Pilate lacked courage to do what was right.

17

Group Activity 1

1. "Father, forgive them, for they don't know what they're doing."
2. "I promise you, today you'll be with me in paradise."
3. "Woman, here is your son. John, here is your mother."
4. "I am thirsty."
5. "My God! My God! Why have you left me?"
6. "It is finished!"

Five Happenings

1. Jesus handed his spirit over to the Father.
2. The curtain in the temple was torn in two.
3. The earth shook.
4. Rocks split apart.
5. Graves were opened.

Fill in the Blanks

1. Simon
2. Cyrene North
3. Golgotha
4. Calvary
5. middle

lonely

Names of God

18

Group Activity 1

5	3
2	1
8	4
6	7
10	9

A Character Sketch

1) rich
2) member of the council
3) secret follower of Jesus

4) didn't agree with the decision to condemn Jesus
5) afraid of Jewish authorities

What Is Love?

This is how we know what love is: Christ gave his life for us. We too ought to give our lives for our brothers!

Love in Action

share, give, welcome, forgive, care

19

Group Activity 1

1. visit
2. spices
3. huge
4. terrified
5. risen
6. Galilee
7. nonsense
8. John
9. believed
10. Magdalene
11. angels
12. peace
13. worship
14. Father

Read a Message

Because Jesus lives we can receive his gift of eternal life!

Jesus Is Lord

Promise	*Demand*
God will live with us	Love God; obey God's teachings
Gives what is asked for	Ask according to God's will
Gives rest to weary	Come to Jesus when tired
Remain in Jesus' love	Love each other
Eternal life	Believe in Jesus

20

Group Activity 1

1. c
2. a
3. c
4. d
5. a
6. a, c
7. b
8. b, c
9. a
10. a, c
11. b, c
12. a

A Verse to Remember

Your word is a lamp to guide me and a light for my path. Psalm 119:105

Why

Jesus came to give his life for us.

21

Group Activity 1

1. Jerusalem
2. terror
3. afraid
4. fish
5. Peace
6. ghost
7. Thomas
8. flesh, bones
9. Scriptures
10. joy
11. witnesses
12. Holy Spirit
13. doubter believer
14. Messiah
15. message, forgiveness

Holy Spirit

John 14:16—stays with us
2 Corinthians 3:6b—gives life
John 14:26—teaches
Acts 1:8—gives power
John 16:13—guides and reveals the truth
Romans 8:16—tells us we are God's children
Romans 8:14—leads

God's Spirit

changes you
is powerful
always with you
helps you work

Dial a Verse

But when the Holy Spirit comes upon you, you will be filled with power, and you will be witnesses for me in Jerusalem, in all Judea and Samaria, and to the ends of the earth. Acts 1:8.

22

Group Activity 1

2, 6, 8, 10

Right or Wrong?

1. a
2. b
3. a, b
4. b
5. a
6. a

Faithful Followers

1. Thomas
2. Moses
3. Philip
4. Nicodemus
5. Peter
6. Joseph
7. Elizabeth
8. Abraham
9. Isaiah
10. Jacob
11. Job
12. Joshua
13. Esther
14. Elijah
15. Daniel
16. Simeon
17. Samuel
18. Stephen

23

Group Activity 1

1. Go to all parts of the world.
2. Preach good news of God's rule.
3. Make disciples of every nation.
4. Baptize new disciples.
5. Teach them to obey my commandments.

Who Am I?

1. Barabbas
2. Second thief
3. Jesus
4. Mary
5. Peter
6. Judas
7. Jesus
8. Peter, James, John
9. Peter
10. Disciples
11. Peter
12. Pilate
13. Pilate's wife
14. Mary Magdalene
15. Cleopas
16. Thomas
17. Peter
18. Joseph of Arimathea

Jesus' Promise

Remember, I am with you always, until the end of time.

24

Group Activity 1

Jesus.

What Is the Word Like?

1. always existed
2. was with God
3. was God
4. light
5. everything created through him

What Has He Done?

1. created life
2. light of humankind
3. came into the world
4. came to his own
5. became a person
6. lived among people on earth
7. showed what God is like

What's in It for You?

1. You have the power to become a child of God.
2. You can know what God is like.

Characteristics of God

all knowing
righteous judge
shelter
forgives
keeps promises
love
strength
slow to anger
gracious
doesn't play favorites

Search for a Message

Jesus came to show us what God is like.